RATIONAL EXUBERANCE

ALSO BY MICHAEL J. MANDEL

The High-Risk Society
The Coming Internet Depression

RATIONAL EXUBERANCE

SILENCING THE ENEMIES OF GROWTH
AND WHY THE FUTURE IS BETTER THAN YOU THINK

Michael J. Mandel

HarperBusiness
An Imprint of HarperCollins*Publishers*

HarperCollins books may be purchased for educational, business, or sales promotional use. For information, please write: Special Markets Department, HarperCollins Publishers Inc., 10 East 53rd Street, New York, NY 10022.

FIRST EDITION

Designed by Jordan Rosenblum

Library of Congress Cataloging-in-Publication Data
Mandel, Michael J.
    Rational exuberance: silencing the enemies of growth and why the future is better than you think / Michael J. Mandel.–1st ed.
        p.   cm.
    Includes index.
    ISBN 0-06-058049-6
    1. United States–Economic conditions–2001–   2. Technological innovations–Economic aspects–United States.   3. Economic forecasting–United States.   4. Economic development.   I. Title.
HC106.83.M36   2004
330.973–dc22   2004040592

04   05   06   07   08   DIX/RRD   10   9   8   7   6   5   4   3   2   1

TO JUDY

CONTENTS

Acknowledgments

I'd like to express my appreciation for my friends and colleagues at *BusinessWeek* for sustaining an environment conducive to serious journalism through the boom and the bust. Allan Sloan and Chris Farrell get my thanks for being willing to engage in endless discussions with me. My editor at HarperCollins, Leah Spiro, deserves credit for terrific suggestions that made the book much better, while Marion Maneker gets my thanks for his willingness to believe in the book. Thanks to my agent, Sarah Chalfant, for stepping up to the plate when needed. And my heartfelt love and appreciation goes to my wife, Judy Scherer, and our children, Elliot and Laura, for supporting me through the book and through life.

Prologue

This book is the result of a decade of reporting, writing, and thinking about economic growth. I was one of the first journalists, or economists for that matter, to observe in the mid-1990s that the U.S. had entered an era of a "New Economy." For me, what made this a "New Economy" was the combination of technology and finance, which drove faster growth while creating more volatility at the same time.

This two-headed notion of the New Economy–faster growth and more volatility–was first outlined in my 1996 book, *The High Risk Society: Peril and Promise in the New Economy*. The theme of technology-driven growth was further developed in a series of cover stories that I wrote as the economics editor and later chief economist at *BusinessWeek*, including the 1997 story entitled "The New Business Cycle." Then my September 2000 book, *The Coming Internet Depression*, warned that the tech and finance downturn was going to be far worse than expected, but could be followed by a new era of innovation.

Let me lay my cards on the table: I am an avid partisan for economic growth. And not just any kind of growth–what I seek is a continuation of the sort of growth we saw in the 1990s, driven by technological breakthroughs that open up whole new vistas of possibilities. This is what I call "exuberant" growth.

Such technology-driven growth is essential, I believe, if we are not to drown in our own problems. The Internet is terrific, but by itself it's not enough to power growth for the next 30 years. Without breakthroughs in medical science, it won't be possible to supply health care to a generation of aging Americans without bankrupting the young. Without breakthroughs in energy production and distribution, it won't be possible to bring Third World countries up to industrialized living standards without badly damaging the environment and stripping the world of natural resources. Without rapid economic growth powered by new technologies, it won't be possible to reduce poverty or to ensure the next generation a better life than we have.

How can I be so sure of this? The lessons of history are very clear. Over the long run, economic progress in an advanced country such as the U.S. depends mainly on technological progress. It was a succession of innovations—including electricity, the telephone, radio, automobile, and antibiotics—that revolutionized life in the early part of the 20th century. Conversely, it was the failure of an important innovation—nuclear power—that helped make the energy crisis of the 1970s worse than it had to be. Similarly, it is not a coincidence that the rise of the Internet in the 1990s coincided with the biggest rise in household incomes, and the biggest drop in poverty, in 30 years. Innovation is indispensable.

ECONOMIC TRAVESTY

For all these reasons, support for technology should be central to economic policy. Unfortunately, technology rarely makes an appearance, either in Washington economic policy discussions or in the textbooks used to teach economics to college students. True, economists have been forced to accept the usefulness of computers and the Internet. Nevertheless, for the most part they remain profoundly ambivalent or even hostile toward most areas of technology. They grudgingly acknowledge the importance of technological change, but they don't understand it or trust it.

This is the single biggest failure of modern economics. In their policy recommendations, most economists were and to a large extent still are obsessed with the budget deficit, despite well-known econometric results suggesting that plausible shifts in budget deficits or surpluses will have little effect on long-term growth–perhaps adding a couple of tenths of a percentage point or so to the long-run growth rate, hardly enough to measure. Meanwhile, the same economic experts have given short shift to fairly obvious measures that could have a much more significant effect on long-term growth, including boosting R&D spending and increasing scholarship funding for advanced science and engineering degrees.

The textbooks are even worse. Most of the best-selling textbooks on economics principles–including those from the best-known economists–downplay any mention of technology. All across the country, Econ 101 students are being taught very little about the importance of technology for growth. That's a travesty.

Take a look at the 2004 edition of the best-known textbook on macroeconomics principles, written by N. Gregory Mankiw (the Harvard professor currently serving as head of George W. Bush's Council of Economic Advisers). In his textbook, "technological knowledge" is listed, briefly, as the fourth (!) determinant of productivity, coming after physical capital, human capital, and natural resources. Any student reading the textbook and preparing for the final exam would be perfectly justified in treating technology as a minor aside. No wonder there's little popular support for boosting spending on R&D.

This hostility to technology helps explain why many economists were so slow to accept the idea of the New Economy in the mid-1990s. At the time, there was a solid core of academic economists, with the highest of reputations, who were insulting and disdainful of the idea that the United States had entered an era of technology-driven growth. Princeton economist Alan Blinder–

who had recently finished serving as vice chairman of the Federal Reserve–wrote in the *Atlantic Monthly* in December 1997:

> Our highly productive future may be a long way off. In the meantime, we may be condemned to a lengthy and uncomfortable transition period.

Around the same time, Paul Krugman, then an economist at the Massachusetts Institute of Technology and now a *New York Times* columnist, refused to even acknowledge the possibility that new technology could push the U.S. growth rate up to 3.5 percent or more:

> The conventional view that the economy has a "speed limit" of around 2-percent to 2.5-percent growth does not come out of thin air . . . I can't bring myself to endorse a doctrine that I know to be just plain dumb.

Of course, this pessimistic view, widely held among economists at the time, turned out to be wrong.

ENEMIES OF GROWTH

In my view, many prominent economists–including Krugman, Blinder, and Mankiw–have in effect been "enemies of growth"–at least the exuberant, technology-driven variety of growth. This may seem a bit harsh, and of course, they would vigorously deny it. But based on what they communicated to noneconomists, through textbooks and public policy pronouncements, the characterization is fair. By underplaying the importance of technology, such economists undermined public support for the economy's main engine of growth. This was a mistake.

To be fair, economists are not the only enemies of growth. For many years, I assumed that achieving rapid economic growth was an objective shared by almost everyone, aside from a few die-hard curmudgeons and environmentalists. After all, faster economic growth raises living standards and provides more resources for everything in society.

I was wrong. Surprisingly, sometimes it seems like there are far more enemies of growth than there are supporters. Over the last few years, I've come to the realization that the consensus for growth—and especially for technology-driven growth—is far weaker than I thought. People say they want growth, but they don't like what comes along with it.

In particular, both on the left and on the right, there is a profound discomfort with technological change. Technology is blamed for creating inequality and unemployment, for corrupting the young with Internet pornography, for flooding our computers with spam, for destroying the environment, for opening up the door to immoral activities such as human cloning, for leading to unproductive financial bubbles, for creating a generation of amoral couch potatoes playing video games. And the advisors who should be the proponents of technology-led growth—the economists—have abnegated their responsibility. Instead, they have chosen to fret endlessly about budget deficits that their own research shows are not much of a problem.

In fact, it's hard to find true friends of growth in either political party. Republicans, for the most part, are fervently in favor of tax cuts or deficit reductions. The Democrats seem to have reconstituted themselves as the party of fiscal responsibility and increased spending on social programs.

In Washington, technology-driven growth is the poor stepchild, receiving a microscopic amount of time, energy, and money from politicians. Government R&D spending, outside of health care and defense, has fallen as a share of gross domestic product since the mid-1990s. The number of science and engineering Ph.D.s received by U.S. citizens is at its lowest level in at least a decade. Meanwhile, politicians unwisely spend their time attacking things like stock options, which helped build Silicon Valley and the U.S. high-tech sector.

Perhaps this shouldn't surprise me. Exuberant, technology-driven growth is upsetting to the status quo, and to the big companies and political donors that benefit from keeping things as they are. Technology represents a force for change that is profoundly threatening.

A NEW POLITICS?

What's needed are a new set of goals for running economic policy, and a new set of politicians brave enough to support them. The goals are threefold:

- Enthusiastic support for technology-driven growth
- Economic security for everyone
- A willingness to embrace the politics of innovation and exuberance

First, I believe that it's necessary to do everything that we can to encourage technological change. That means far more attention must be paid to encouraging basic and applied research, the formation and funding of innovative start-ups, and the development of the most skilled workforce possible. Conversely, there needs to be far less debate about the budget and trade deficits, and more of an understanding that America's greatness has always rested on its ability to change, to embrace technology.

For that reason, I also advocate a heretical macroeconomic policy. For the last 50 years, the main goal of macroeconomists has been to smooth out both the ups and downs of the business cycle. It's still paramount to avoid deep recessions; however, I believe that technology-driven booms, like the one of the 1990s, should be encouraged. Although running the economy "hot" does carry dangers—namely, the possibility of a bust afterward—the advantages of providing better conditions for innovation and for risk-taking more than outweigh the downsides.

But such growth-oriented policies are unworkable without an equally intent focus on providing more economic security as well. Rapid technological change is inherently threatening to people, because it has the potential to destroy their jobs and overturn their way of life.

Therefore, exuberant growth must go hand in hand with economic security. We must give Americans better information about the financial and technological risks that they are facing. We must give them better tools for managing their own risks. And above all, we must strengthen the safety net to allow Americans to support technology-driven growth without worrying that it will put them in the poorhouse.

In this new world, a new political coalition is needed, built around both pro-growth policies and policies that promote economic security and fairness. The coalition will cut across party lines, encompassing all the groups that benefit from technology-driven growth: the investors with money in the stock market, the educated managers and professionals who thrive in periods of rapid change, the less-skilled workers who can ride a boom to a better life.

Finally, and perhaps most important, we must embrace the exuberance brought on by new technologies, and renounce the ethic that too much growth is bad for us. Exuberance is not a character flaw; it's not something that has to be rooted out. Rather, it's the essential motive force for a technologically vibrant economy.

How do we know that these new possibilities will exist in the future? How do we know that the uncertainty and turmoil of exuberant growth will pay off? One reason is the record of history. Every time in the past that the pessimists thought that innovation had stalled out, they were proven wrong. Similarly, economists who thought that the U.S. economy had reached a mature state in the 1980s were proven wrong as well by the Internet and the tech boom.

We do not know what lies beyond the next hill. It cannot be proven that there are new opportunities beyond the horizon. But if we do not have faith, we will never find out.

Glossary of Key Concepts

EXUBERANT GROWTH

Economic expansion driven in large part by new technologies and innovations. Tends to be significantly faster, accompanied by rising living standards and higher stock prices, on average. Also tends to be more unpredictable, more volatile, and more exciting.

CAUTIOUS GROWTH

Economic expansion based mainly on the steady accumulation of physical and (sometimes) human capital, rather than technological change. Tends to be slower than exuberant growth and more predictable.

CAPITAL FUNDAMENTALISTS

Economists who behave as if savings and investment in physical and (sometimes) human capital are the only forces driving growth. Generally ignore or minimize the role of technology. Focus on reducing the government budget deficit as the principal route to faster economic growth.

HIGH-PERFORMANCE FINANCIAL SYSTEM

A financial system able to easily fund high-risk, high-return ventures such as start-ups and investment in new technologies. Also capable of handling booms and busts without overheating or freezing up.

PULSATING MARKETS

Financial markets that generate a series of bubbles, each one corresponding to a different new technology. Can serve as a potent stimulus for innovation, while exposing investors to high volatility.

PRO-GROWTH POLICIES

Policies designed to directly encourage technology-driven growth. Include increases in government spending on basic and early stage applied research and higher education. Also includes encouragement of market financing for innovation, such as venture capital and stock options.

TRANSPARENCY

A policy of increasing the amount of information available about corporate and government activities. Makes it harder to lie to people, and harder to take advantage of them. Essential for maintaining trust in risky financial markets.

INCOME INSURANCE

A policy of offering Americans more protection against sudden changes in income. Includes adjusting the tax code to allow income averaging, which would give a big tax refund to workers who lose their jobs. Would make it easier for Americans to take risks.

FORTIFYING THE SAFETY NET

A policy of strengthening the protection against job loss. Includes improving health care coverage for the unemployed. Would be much easier to pay for such programs when growth is rapid.

POPPING OF THE EDUCATION BUBBLE

A possible sharp fall in the real wages of college-educated workers. Could happen if innovation slows in the U.S., and if the global supply of college-educated workers keeps increasing. Would represent a break from two decades of rising incomes for the U.S. educated elite.

CHAPTER 1

In Defense of
Exuberance

We are building a bridge to future prosperity. The first pylon–
information technology–is in place. The question now is whether
we will have the will and capability to finish the span.

Each of the great industrial revolutions of the past was built on
multiple technological breakthroughs, not just one. The late 19th
and early 20th centuries, for example, saw the invention and widespread usage of electricity, the internal combustion engine and the
automobile, the telephone, the radio, antibiotics, the factory assembly line, and the airplane. All together, these innovations led to
an unprecedented rise in global living standards.

So far the latest burst of innovation has produced just one
breakthrough of equivalent importance–the microprocessor, the
foundation of the entire Information Revolution. Gaining power
and speed each year, the microprocessor has created entire new in-

dustries, and revolutionized the transmission and manipulation of information. The rise of information technology propelled the economic boom of the 1990s, and continues to propel rapid productivity growth today.

But today's advances in information technology–no matter how potent–get us only part of the way to where we need to be. In the short run, the U.S. needs to keep innovating if it is to maintain a vibrant economy, a strong job market, a rising stock market, and a high standard of living.

A slowdown in innovation also drains away the main competitive advantage of the U.S. When technologies become routine, they become much easier to move to low-wage countries. Routine programming and call centers get shifted to India, manufacturing gets moved to China, and there are no new industries to take their place.

Without innovation, we'll see the collapse of the demand for high-paid college-educated workers, who are far more valuable in a rapidly innovating economy; an explosion of budget deficits on the federal, state, and local levels; and a lagging stock market. Perhaps most significant, a technologically stagnant U.S. would find it harder to project its military power abroad, without tightening its belt at home.

In the long term, there are tough problems that can only be solved with breakthroughs in areas besides information technology. Two in particular stand out. First, we need to figure out how to provide good medical care to the retiring baby boom generation, without either bankrupting the younger population or rationing medical care. This will require radical medical advances, matching antibiotics and vaccines in importance.

On a global level, if the populations in China or India approach anywhere close to the living standards of the advanced countries, there will be tremendous pressure on world energy supplies. Right now each person in China consumes one-fifth of the energy used per person in the advanced nations, including industrial usage, and each person in India consumes one-tenth the energy. If energy usage per person in India and China rise to even half the level of industrialized countries, we will need major breakthroughs in energy technology either to find new sources of nonpolluting energy or to substantially reduce usage.

THE GOOD NEWS

This book will argue that it is rational to be optimistic about the next decade and about the future beyond—if we are willing to commit ourselves to innovation-driven, or what we will call *exuberant,* growth. There are plenty of potential new technological breakthroughs simmering beneath the surface. To name just a few: solar power that is competitive with conventional energy sources; biotech advances that actually cut health care costs; nanotechnology (building useful objects atom by atom), which changes the nature of manufacturing and actually makes it cost-effective to produce things in the U.S. again. None of these new technologies is ready for prime time yet, but there's a very good chance that at least one of them will be ready to pay off big over the next 10 years.

In addition, the commitment to research and development (R&D) has been expanding around the world. The U.S. has been the leader, with private-sector R&D spending as a share of GDP (gross domestic product) up sharply since the mid-1990s, more than making up for the relative weakness in government spending. Japan, and the European Union, too, have continued to boost R&D spending, despite stagnant economies. In Asia, Chinese R&D expenditures now exceed those of any of the European countries, according to the latest figures from the OECD (Organization for

Economic Co-operation and Development) while India is in the top 10 worldwide. Korea, Taiwan, and Singapore also dramatically increased R&D spending in the 1990s. All of these resources contribute to the global ability to innovate.

The commitment to higher education, too, is much stronger than it has ever been. The U.S. still is a leader there as well, with more than half of the adult population having some form of tertiary (post–high school) education.

At the same time, enrollments and the number of college graduates have been rising in Europe and Asia, as it's become clear that college is where people learn how to work independently, solve ambiguous problems, and acquire all the other advanced skills necessary to prosper in a fast-changing world. In India, for example, the number of colleges for professional education (including technical and engineering) doubled between 1994 and 2001, according to statistics from India's Department of Education. After several years of massive expansions in enrollment, China had 2.1 million new college graduates in 2003, surpassing 1.3 million in new college graduates in the U.S. What's more, the number of new college graduates in China is expected to rise to 2.8 million in 2004, according to China's Ministry of Personnel.

THE FINANCIAL EDGE

The global expansion in R&D spending and higher education is both boon and bane for the U.S. On the one hand, more smart people working on new ideas is likely to increase the global rate of innovation. That raises the odds that at least one of the new technologies will take flight over the next decade. And since ideas and innovations flow relatively easily across national borders, research done elsewhere will benefit the U.S. as well.

On the other hand, the U.S. no longer has the commanding position in R&D and level of education that it once had. There is real competition out there for the American educated class, raising the threat that the 20-year boom for college-educated workers may be coming to an end.

Indeed, there are substantial weaknesses in the U.S.'s approach to innovation that need to be addressed. Defense and health account for about 80 percent of the federal government's spending on R&D, squeezing out critical areas such as energy. And the number of graduate degrees in science and engineering going to Americans has plummeted in recent years. Funding for both R&D and graduate science education must be increased substantially.

The U.S., though, does possess a unique competitive advantage: the first *high-performance* financial system the world has ever known. During boom times, the U.S. is able to fund innovative and growing new businesses with financial instruments–venture capital and junk bonds–that barely exist anywhere else. And then when the inevitable bust comes, the U.S. financial system is highly liquid and far more diversified than elsewhere, able to cope with sharp plunges without freezing up.

Over the last few years, it was still remarkably easy for corporations to issue bonds and for homeowners to get mortgages, despite one of the deepest market declines in history, multiple corporate defaults, and continuing news of corruption. Even the venture capital and initial public offering markets have begun to recover from the deep tech bust.

In historical context, the U.S. high-performance financial system represents a real leap forward. What people often forget is that what distinguishes capitalism from other economic systems is how it handles "capital." The stock and bond markets developed in the 19th century to fund massive capital-intensive projects such as the construction of the railroads, the electricity network, and large industrial plants. But never before has there been a financial system that provided a way of systematically funding cutting-edge research and innovation.

For the U.S., the ability to direct resources to innovative new businesses sucks in new ideas and smart people from all over the world. That accelerates innovation, produces new jobs, and creates a competitive advantage that other countries cannot match, no matter how low their wages are.

By comparison, the financial systems elsewhere are far weaker. Japan and continental Europe are still struggling, for the most part, with sclerotic bank-based finance, which makes it much easier for money to flow to existing big companies than to smaller, more innovative ones. The Chinese financial system is rickety, and a potential weak spot for an otherwise booming economy. And India's stock market is tiny next to the New York Stock Exchange. Financial institutions are far more difficult to duplicate than technology.

A TOUGH SELL

Our optimism about growth, though, has to be tempered with some realism: Exuberant growth is a surprisingly tough sell. Innovation and technological change have legions of enemies, at every point along the political spectrum, from the left to the right. It's not just the technological Luddites. Liberals worry about the job loss and income inequality created by new technologies. Environmentalists worry about global warming and the negative impact of genetically modified food. Conservatives worry about Internet pornography and the ethical impact of stem cell research.

In addition, many people, of all stripes, are concerned that the headlong rush toward "newness" obscures more important values such as contact with friends and family. "We excel at making a living but often fail at making a life. We celebrate our prosperity but yearn for purpose," writes social psychologist David Myers, who wrote the 2000 book *The American Paradox.* "We cherish our freedoms but long for connection. In an age of plenty, we feel spiritual hunger."

Economists—who should be the biggest fans of fast growth—have mostly shown themselves to be opposed or indifferent to technological change. In their textbooks, popular writings, and public policy pronouncements, technology has been for the most part ignored or dismissed by leading economists such as N. Gregory Mankiw, chairman of George Bush's Council of Economic Advisers, and Paul Krugman, the *New York Times* columnist. It's almost as if they were living in a parallel universe, where innovation was not the main driving force behind growth, and only the budget deficit counted.

To put it another way, what might be called the Silicon Valley mentality—favoring experimentation, innovation, change—faces a hostile climate today. Most people are uncomfortable with the sort of uncertainty and risk that technology entrepreneurs live with daily. There's no way of knowing which technology or which company is going to succeed and which will fail. Innovation requires abandoning the caution and prudence that is second nature to many of us, and taking a leap into the unknown. Innovation is not fair—some people get rich, while others lose their jobs.

One of the clearest signs of the hostility to innovation is the attack on stock options. There's no disputing that the tech sector has been the most innovative part of the U.S. economy, able to outcompete tough foreign rivals. There's also no disputing that tech companies have been the most aggressive users of broad-based stock options. Start-up companies use them to attract the most creative and innovative workers by offering them a piece of the action, while larger companies such as Cisco use them to motivate their workforce.

Nevertheless, as this book is being written, the Financial Accounting Standards Board is formulating rules that would make it much more expensive for all companies—the tech sector included—to issue stock options. This does address the real problem of CEOs bulking up their pay with mammoth stock option grants that have little risk attached. However, a broad-brush action against stock options seems distinctly counterproductive, at a time when the U.S. is concerned about competing against China and India. The phrase "cutting off your nose to spite your face" comes to mind.

In many ways a backlash against innovation is entirely understandable. Even people who are not averse to change or growth have been scarred by the last 10 years of boom and bust. This period of exuberant growth—stellar in so many ways—has left behind scars. Part of those, of course, are the result of the bust. The sharp drop in the value of investment portfolios, the loss of jobs, the legions of dot-coms gone sour, the corporate bankruptcies and scandals have all seared themselves into people's minds. It is difficult to remember what was good about the last 10 years when you or a spouse is out of a job and your mortgage is coming due.

On top of that, even the boom years were quite stressful for many people. Rapid change and innovation, however beneficial, imposed its own costs. People suffered from "upgrade exhaustion." Every day they had to deal with new products and new ways of doing things or risk being left behind. The very forces driving growth during the 1990s—technological change, deregulation, and globalization—required people and companies to take more risks, and to accept more insecurity.

That's why, for many people, another round of exuberant growth doesn't seem so attractive. It only seems natural to want to slow down and get comfortable, rather than being forced to adapt all the time. As one columnist wrote in the *Wall Street Journal* in August 2003: "Why can't we just settle into 'slow and steady'?"

WHAT COULD GO WRONG?

It is not inevitable that exuberant growth will triumph over its enemies. In fact, in most historical periods, the opponents of innovation have succeeded in dampening technological change. As economic historian Joel Mokyr writes in his 1990 book, *The Lever of Riches:*

> Technological progress is like a fragile and vulnerable plant, whose flourishing is not only dependent on the appropriate surrounding and climate, but whose life is almost always short. It is highly sensitive to the social and economic environment and can easily be arrested by relatively small external changes.

What happens if Americans cannot be persuaded that exuberant growth is in their interest? What happens if the confidence that allowed and encouraged us to take risks in the 1990s ebbs away? What happens if we retreat from the future?

The outcome of such a path would be much slower, less turbulent growth for the U.S. economy—what we might call *cautious growth.* This would involve much less risk-taking and much more attention to security. Companies would focus on boosting their margins, rather than taking chances on developing new products or technologies. Workers would treasure the solidity of their current jobs, rather than taking chances on jumping to a start-up in return for the possibility of getting rich. And investors would look far more skeptically on new public companies or start-ups that need money.

The result of cautious growth would look much like the economies of European countries such as France and Germany, where social stability is valued over change, and where there is strong support for prudence and caution in dealing with innovations such as genetically modified crops and Internet privacy regulations. These two countries in particular have managed a growth rate of only 2.2 percent and 1.3 percent, respectively, between 1995 and 2003. That was far less than the U.S. and slow enough to push their unemployment rate above 9 percent.

If the U.S. shifted to cautious growth, the most pernicious and surprising effect would be the *popping of the education bubble*. During the 1990s, college-educated workers thrived because the fast pace of innovation demanded workers who could learn and adapt quickly to new technologies. That drove up pay for educated workers, widening the gap between them and their less-educated counterparts.

But if the pace of innovation slows, there will be much less need for college-educated workers. Jobs will be routinized, and companies will replace expensive college-educated workers with cheaper workers with associate degrees or even less. Moreover, there is a flood of new college graduates entering the workplace, both in the U.S. and overseas. Falling demand and rising supply means a sharp downturn in the incomes and fortunes of the college-educated, at least for a few years.

If the U.S. follows the path of cautious growth, the bursting of the education bubble is going to be the seminal political and economic event of the next several years. College-educated workers get almost half of all wage payments, so as their situation worsens, so will consumer spending. The political landscape will dramatically change, since educated voters will not support the status quo, as they did in the 2002 election.

The transition from exuberant to cautious growth will be accompanied by other malevolent side effects as well. As income growth slows, it will become a lot harder to service all the debt that companies and people took on during the 1990s. Housing prices will slump, and perhaps even plummet. And governments will have trouble raising enough money to fund retirement and medical programs.

The real danger is that once the U.S. moves away from exuberant growth, it will be hard to get back again. The antigrowth arguments will seem quite persuasive to members of the educated class, who for the first time in decades will be having a tough time finding jobs. It will be tempting to reject the risk-taking and the technological innovation, to reject globalization, to reject the financial markets.

The technology will still be there, the faster computers, the higher-capacity communication gear. But the will to use them in new and different ways, to experiment, will be much less. It will be a vicious cycle—the more cautious Americans become, the less innovation we will have, and the slower growth we will get. And that, in turn, will make Americans even more cautious. The result will be an ossification of our economic arteries, an economic aging that cannot be reversed.

BUILDING SUPPORT FOR EXUBERANCE

It's easy to make a purely economic case for exuberant growth, because new technologies are the key to long-term increases in income and living standards. Moreover, the shift to cautious growth will result in lower incomes and lost jobs for a lot of people.

But such economically based reasoning is not compelling to the opponents of exuberant growth, for two reasons. First, the average American already enjoys a per capita GDP an order of magnitude greater than that of a country such as Indonesia. With U.S. homes getting larger and larger, and obesity one of the biggest health problems, it's hard to explain why it's so important for most Americans to have more income. Second, most of the arguments against exuberant growth–for example, inequality or Internet pornography–are not economic in nature.

Thus, if we want to maintain the consensus for innovation, we must be willing to address some of the noneconomic objections to exuberant growth. Moreover, we must actually explain why it is that exuberant growth and innovation make for a better and more enjoyable society, above and beyond the economic effects.

An innovative economy demands the willingness to experiment, the ability to take risks and commit money into promising opportunities, and the intestinal fortitude to fail and keep going. But it can't all be tough slogging. An innovative economy can't be sustained unless people can enjoy the periods of exuberance and expanded possibilities when an innovation takes flight, as the Internet did in the 1990s. The right balance between pain and pleasure is essential.

MAKING EXUBERANCE MORE ACCEPTABLE

What would be needed to make exuberant growth more acceptable to people? If we can do that, we can have the best of both worlds. We will be able to run the economy hot enough to generate new waves of innovation and growth, while keeping the stress of change down to tolerable levels.

If we want people to take risks during the boom, they have to be reassured that there is a level playing field, and that there isn't critical information being hidden from them. In effect, we need to move toward *transparency*–providing as much information as possible to everyone.

The Securities and Exchange Commission (SEC) has been prodding companies to do that, but an economy that runs on risk-taking requires a lot more. For example, it may be necessary to force corporations to disclose more details of their investments and employment outside the U.S., an essential piece of information in an era where globalization is key. It may also be helpful for corporations to make their tax returns public. That big step–which in fact was the way that the corporate income tax was originally implemented–will ensure that investors and workers have a better understanding of the financial condition of the company, rather than the sanitized version that appears in the annual reports. Access to Enron's tax returns, for example, would have made it much easier for outsiders to catch the company's financial shenanigans.

Next, we have to ease the pain for Americans who are hit by financial or technological turbulence. In an ideal world, the government would be able to provide some form of *income insurance,* which would go beyond unemployment insurance and offer a measure of protection against drops in income. That would make people feel easier about taking risks.

There have been previous attempts to set up income insurance programs. Notably, the Trade Act of 2002 makes a start by setting up a pilot program to offer wage insurance for older, low-wage workers displaced by trade and forced to take even lower-paying jobs. Qualified workers can get up to half the difference between their old and new wages, up to $10,000 over two years.

However, there's also a straightforward way to use the tax system to accomplish the same purpose, by allowing people to utilize *income averaging* over several years for tax purposes. As in the case of public corporate tax returns, this is something that was once provided for in the tax laws but has been taken out. Income averaging would mean that someone who did well one year, and then poorly the next, could average over the two years and end up paying a lower tax rate. The result would be a big tax refund for people–especially middle- or high-income taxpayers–who have lost their job or been forced to take a lower-paying one.

Finally, it's necessary to *fortify the safety net* for everyone. In a world in which people are exposed to the uncertainty and stress of rapid technological change, we don't want to impose gratuitous risks on anyone. In particular, a fast-growing, exuberant economy has enough resources to provide at least a minimal level of health care coverage for everyone.

THE MORAL JUSTIFICATION FOR GROWTH

There's another compelling reason why the educated class should embrace exuberant growth, warts and all. Exuberant growth broadens our lives, bringing in possibilities and alternatives that were never thought of before, that are completely unexpected. Innovation and technological change broaden the known world, not just in one direction but in many directions. That means new technologies, new ways of organizing work and society, new ways of communicating.

By contrast, cautious growth keeps our lives moving along the same road. Cautious growth is tending to our fields, while exuberant growth is an exploration of what lies beyond the mountains. The outcome of innovation-driven exuberant growth is a set of undetermined possibilities and opportunities in every field of human endeavor–science, art, business, even sports–rather than a fixed and limited goal.

Focusing on innovation engages our energies and allows us to be creative, in a way that is not possible in a slow-growth economy. Exuberant growth creates opportunities for us and our children and allows us to dream. It frees up our politics and gives us the resources to solve problems that are not going to go away.

GLOBAL RESPONSIBILITY

There is an additional moral imperative that falls on the educated elite in the U.S. The U.S. economy is rich enough and big enough to absorb the risks of innovation. The U.S. also has a critical mass of educated people, and a financial system able to fund their ideas. It is our obligation to take risks, to be the trailblazers and absorb most of the uncertainty. We are the only country big enough to absorb a failure on the magnitude of the massive telecom and dotcom losses, without losing a step.

If the U.S. does not walk the path of exuberant growth, there is no one else who will. The fast-growing Asian giants, China and India, don't have the resources or the financial infrastructure to support risky innovation. Japan and Europe have chosen the path of safe, cautious growth, which is based on the steady accumulation of capital. If the U.S. follows suit, the result will be a lower growth rate for the whole world. And without technological innovations that increase productivity and reduce the use of scarce resources, it is hard to see how the mass of the world's population can even approach the standard of living of the industrialized nations.

We should be taking on the big risks. That's the right thing for us to do. And even if they don't work out, that's our responsibility to the rest of the world and to our children. This is not simply a matter of economics. It's a matter of moral responsibility.

Embracing exuberant growth is a way of giving purpose to our lives, over and above the simple accumulation of goods. It's a way of ensuring that our children live not in the Age of Uncertainty but in the Age of Possibility.

CHAPTER 2

The Two Types
of Growth

New products, new industries, and more jobs require
continuous additions to knowledge of the laws of nature,
and the application of that knowledge to practical purposes.

Vannevar Bush

Science, the Endless Frontier, 1945

Is it possible to have economic growth without innovation? In theory (and in most economic textbooks) the answer is yes.

Here's how. Imagine an economy in which companies offer the exact same array of goods and services each year. Department stores would sell the same shirts and dresses each year. Automakers would roll identical Camrys, Explorers, and Cadillacs off the assembly line, with the same choices for colors and options (and run the same ads on TV!). Hospitals would offer patients the same medical treatments for cancer and heart diseases and the like. Pharmacies would sell the same antidepressants and medicines for controlling high blood pressure. Electronics stores would offer the same MP3 players and DVD players, year after year.

Now imagine that each year companies become more efficient and smarter in the way they produce their offerings, so that they can charge lower prices. Just as the price of a good MP3 player has fallen from $300 to $150 over the last several years, the prices of homes, cars, medical care, and all sorts of necessities of life would fall as well, while wages would remain the same.

Such a world would not be deflationary, in the negative sense. Rather, this would be a world of rising productivity and rising living standards. Americans would be better clothed, better fed, better housed. The average person would live longer, as an increasing number of people would be able to get the medical care they needed. The percentage of the population living in poverty would fall, as more and more families would be able to afford the necessities of life.

GROWTH AND INNOVATION

Such a world of growth without innovation is economic nirvana, at least as described in the economic textbooks. There's only one problem—it never happens that way in reality.

The history of the industrialized world—and certainly from the beginning of the 20th century right through to the age of the Internet—shows that growth without innovation is inevitably slow and boring. If you keep making the same items—even with small improvements—the result is stagnation. "Without novel and radical departures," writes Joel Mokyr, "the continuous process of improving and refining existing techniques would run into diminishing returns and eventually peter out."

It's the big leaps into something new that really changes people's lives. It is impossible to imagine what our life would look like without some of the bigger innovations of the last century. A better-made horse-drawn carriage pales beside the development of the automobile. Serious infections are treatable in a way that was not possible before the advent of antibiotics. The telephone, radio, and television dramatically changed the nature of long-range communication.

The list goes on and on. Fast air travel allows us to make trips that were simply inconceivable 100 years ago. Prozac and the anti-depression meds make daily life easier for millions of Americans suffering each day from recurrent depression. The automated teller machine has changed the way we manage the cash in our pocket, while mortgage-backed securities have revolutionized housing finance. The invention of wallboard–preformed plaster walls–by U.S. Gypsum in 1933 made it possible to manufacture walls for homes in a factory at a dramatically lower cost than that of building plaster walls in place. High-yield crops make it possible to feed ever larger populations with less land. And let's not forget Viagra, which has improved the quality of life for many people who would otherwise have to go without.

EXUBERANT GROWTH

A Porsche Boxster and a Toyota Corolla are both cars, but they are so different that no one mistakes one for the other. Similarly, innovation-driven growth is so different from its slow-innovation counterpart that it deserves a different name.

We will call innovation-driven growth *exuberant growth*, because large-scale innovation is usually accompanied by excitement and a sense of exploration and adventure. Whether surfing the Internet, listening to music on a radio for the first time, or even buying their first electric washing machine, people get a rush out of the idea of being able to do something new that they couldn't do before. It's like discovering an unexplored new country.

The sense of excitement can manifest itself in a variety of ways, depending on the innovation. Sometimes it shows up as a nationwide fervor to invest in new companies, and a resulting stock market boom, as it did in the 1920s and the 1990s. Sometimes an innovative new product is so immediately compelling to consumers that it triggers a massive buying wave, as in the case of the VCR, which took off in 1982 and by 1990 was in almost 70 percent of households, and in the process revolutionized consumer electronics. And sometimes it just shows as a massive national preoccupation with a single person or adventure. The white-hot media attention in 1927 paid to Charles Lindbergh's solo flight across the Atlantic Ocean reflected the enormous excitement of living in an era where airplanes made such a trip possible.

The early days of electricity, too, brought forth a similar enthusiasm. After Thomas Edison announced that he had invented the first viable lightbulb in 1879, his Menlo Park laboratory became a mecca for "electricity sightseers":

> Each subsequent afternoon and evening, flocks of
> electricity sightseers crowded off specially scheduled
> Pennsylvania Railroad trains, or pulled up in the crudest
> of farm wagons and the most luxurious of broughams . . .
> the visitors would head through the dark toward the bright
> laboratory, there to push through and gaze in awe at the
> magical display.

There's an inherent dramatic intensity present in exuberant growth that is not present in a world of smooth predictable
growth. Almost by definition, the extreme success of each of these
innovations came as surprise–either because the breakthrough
was not imagined beforehand, or it was thought to be too difficult to work on a large scale, or it was believed to be economically
unimportant.

The discovery of Viagra was pure luck, for example. Treating
erectile dysfunction was the unexpected side effect of a drug that
the Pfizer pharmaceutical company was developing to treat heart
disease. Similarly, nobody had any idea that microwaves could be
used to cook food until one researcher at Raytheon discovered that
a candy bar in his pocket had been melted by radar waves.

The ultimate success of even the biggest and most important
innovations is hard to predict. The first microprocessor–with all
the essential "brains" for a computer on a chip–was designed by
Intel in 1971 to power a scientific calculator made by a Japanese
company, to be marketed under the Busicom name. At the time,
neither Intel nor its Japanese customer had any idea of the potential applications. The rights to the microprocessor were originally
sold to the Japanese company, and had to be bought back by Intel.

Exuberance is not about gradual, incremental, slow change.
Joseph Schumpeter of Harvard, in his classic 1942 *Capitalism,
Socialism and Democracy,* observed that economic change is a
"history of revolutions," as the waterwheel is eventually replaced
by the modern power plant, or the mail coach is replaced by the
airplane. Mokyr identified what he called "macroinventions," or
"those inventions in which a radical new idea, without clear
precedent, emerges more or less ab nihilo." More recently, Clayton
Christensen, a Harvard Business School professor, wrote about
"disruptive innovations"–new technologies that break the old
model of business, and eventually offer far better performance at

far lower prices. Revolutions and disruptions are the name of the game when it comes to exuberant growth.

CAUTIOUS GROWTH

The opposite of exuberant growth is *cautious growth*. Cautious growth is built on incremental improvements in the existing structure of the economy, combined with a steady accumulation of physical, human, and intellectual capital. A manufacturing company buys a slightly newer and faster version of a machine it already has; workers get a bit more education and training, to become more productive; corporate research scientists develop improved versions of existing products.

Cautious growth is based on the prudent virtues of saving and investing wisely for the future. This is an idea which is very familiar to all of us. Like planting a seed, individuals, corporations, and governments can choose to spend their money and resources in ways that will bear fruit in later years. That eventually translates into more output and faster growth.

It makes sense that as the amount of physical capital–machinery, computers, software, and the like–grows, the productive capabilities of a society grow as well. Similarly, as a society's human capital–the education and training of its workers–increases, so does its potential output. Better-educated and -trained workers are more capable, and better able to handle sophisticated equipment and more complicated tasks.

Increasing physical and human capital requires a sacrifice–output that could have been consumed is invested for the future instead. If you go to college instead of working, it means that you are building up debts rather than earning money. If a country invests heavily in new machinery and equipment, that generally requires resources that could have been used to improve living standards in the short run.

There's a certain satisfying primeval predictability about cautious growth. You reap what you sow—the more you save and invest, the faster the economy grows. Conversely, if you consume too much, or run big budget deficits, the economy suffers. Cautious growth rewards the prudent and punishes the profligate.

For the most part, large corporations practice cautious growth. They focus on their "core competencies"—the things that they already do well. They avoid investments and projects that are too risky.

The epitome of cautious growth is the suggestion box. Changes are small, gradual, incremental. The goal is to become more efficient at doing current tasks, and better at serving existing markets and customers. Rearrange the assembly line so that workers need to take fewer steps; fine-tune the back office so that paperwork takes less time.

Together, these efforts create a steady forward momentum of cautious growth, which doesn't require any big breakthroughs. Cautious growth does not involve any sharp breaks or disruptions. It's far easier to describe or predict than exuberant growth, and far more dependable. It's as if we are moving along a straight or gently winding road, where we can easily see what's ahead. In the phrase that became common during the tech bust, there is "good visibility."

RUNNING THE NUMBERS

At any time the U.S. economy has strands of both exuberant and cautious growth. Companies are trying to create new products and master breakthrough technologies, even as they are improving the products already on the market. Most of the activities that we engage in each day fall under the heading of cautious growth.

Can we measure how much innovation adds to growth? The answer is yes, with caveats. The first thing to realize is that growth, as measured by the government, is a fairly recent concept. True, calculations of national income and spending go back to the 1600s, mainly intended as a way of assessing the military potential of potential enemies (for example, a 17th-century English statistician produced estimates comparing the performance of the Dutch and the French economies). There were intermittent attempts in Britain and elsewhere to measure national income from the beginning of the 1700s to the 1930s, but there was little comparability over time, so it was hard to assess growth rates.

The U.S. was actually the leader in calculating annual figures for real growth–that is, adjusted for inflation. Even here, the annual growth figures only became a regular event starting in 1942. That's very recent, considering how important growth is to the U.S. and to the economy.

Coming up with an overall growth rate for an economy is a far more complicated process than it seems at first. In particular, it's necessary to decide what aspects of the economy to include in the gross domestic product (GDP), and which parts to leave out. Personal consumption, business investment, government spending, exports and imports are all part of the number. The implicit value of housing services from owner-occupied homes are part of national output, as calculated by the Bureau of Economic Analysis. On the other hand, the implicit value of services performed by stay-at-home spouses is not (because they are not part of the "market" economy). Software spending by businesses used to be left out of the output number; now it's included.

This is relevant because many of the most important effects of innovations are actually omitted from today's calculation of the

GDP. For example, health care innovations that add to longevity only affect growth if they increase the ability of people to work. Changes in the quality of life–i.e. the length of time spent commuting to work–are also missed by the statistics, as are the effects of technology on the environment.

A BIG DIFFERENCE

With this in mind, let's make a clear distinction between cautious and exuberant growth. Cautious growth depends on observable and measurable factors. These include the number of workers and the amount of hours they put in; the quality of the workforce, as measured by better education and training (human capital); and the stock of equipment, software, and buildings owned by businesses (physical capital). The size of the workforce, human capital, physical capital–these are the three main inputs to cautious growth.

After we have accounted for these three predictable factors, there's usually quite a bit of growth left to explain. This remainder–usually called the residual, or multifactor productivity, or total factor productivity–is where the effects of technology and innovation would show up.

This calculation was first done in the mid-1950s by Robert Solow, an economist at the Massachusetts Institute of Technology. Solow, who later won the Nobel Prize in Economics for this work, found that the residual, astoundingly, accounted for much more than half of long-term growth of productivity–that is, output per hour.

This result was very controversial at the time, because it seemed to give innovation–which most economists rarely studied– a much bigger role than capital investment in driving growth.

There were two reactions within the economics profession. First, subsequent research did manage to pare down the residual to roughly one-half of long-term productivity growth. Second, there was a tremendous amount of debate over the years about how to interpret the residual. At various points, reputable economists suggested that the large size of the residual was due to mismeasurement or to factors other than innovation.

Still, almost 50 years after Solow's original research, his basic result–that roughly half of productivity growth cannot be explained by capital investment or by human capital–still stands up. Moreover, it's most natural to interpret the residual–as most economists do–as a reflection of the innovativeness of the economy, in terms of both technology and business.

Table 1, below, gives a breakdown of long-term growth in the U.S., as calculated by the Bureau of Labor Statistics (BLS). Between 1948 and 2001, the output of the nonfarm business sector increased by a factor of nearly 7 times. That's equivalent to an average annual growth rate of 3.6 percent a year.

Out of those 3.6 percentage points, 1.4 represent the average annual increase in total hours worked–mostly because of a bigger population. The other 2.2 percentage points come from rising labor productivity, measured as output per hour. To put that in perspective, an average annual increase of 2.2 percent, taken over 53 years, translates into a *tripling* of productivity over that stretch. It's as if a person who could dig one ditch in a day in 1948 could, with the right tools and know-how, dig three today.

Where does that tripling of productivity come from? According to the calculations by the BLS, roughly one-half comes from investment in physical and human capital–machines, software, and education. The other half comes from growth in what the BLS calls multifactor productivity–or, innovation, both technological and business.

TABLE 1: SOURCES OF GROWTH, 1948–2001

	ANNUAL AVERAGE PERCENTAGE CHANGE
Output of nonfarm business sector	3.6
Labor hours	1.4
Output per hour	2.2
Contribution of capital investment	0.8
Contribution of improved labor quality	0.2
Other factors, including technological change	1.1

Source: U.S. Bureau of Labor Statistics (Because of rounding, components of productivity growth do not sum to total.)

Let's put this another way. Without innovation, the long-term growth rate of the U.S. economy would have been closer to 2.5 percent per year than to the 3.6 percent per year that has been the average since World War II. In effect, we can interpret 2.5 percent as being a rough estimate of the long-term rate of cautious growth. Anything above that level of 2.5 percent per year seems to necessarily come from exuberant growth and the effects, direct and indirect, of technological breakthroughs.

SIZING THE IMPACT

Does the difference between 2.5 percent annual growth and 3.6 percent growth really matter? Certainly on a year-by-year basis, 1 percentage point doesn't seem like much. A typical person's weight fluctuates by more than 1 percent over the course of a day (i.e., if you weigh 200 pounds, 1 percent of that is two pounds).

However, when applied to the entire U.S. economy, 1 percent becomes quite significant. One percent of a $11 trillion economy is $110 billion, which would have been enough to pay for the entire cost of the Iraq war in 2003. Over a 10-year period starting from today, an exuberant economy with 3.6 percent annual growth would be about $1.8 trillion bigger in today's dollars than a cautious economy with 2.5 percent growth. To put that in perspective, the entire budget of the federal government today is about $2.4 trillion.

To put it a different way: If the economy had grown at the rate of cautious growth over the last 50 years, it would be 40 percent smaller today. Our living standard would be about 40 percent lower, our houses would be smaller, we'd have much less resources for health care, and there would be many fewer cars on the road.

The message is simple: Over the long run, the evidence shows that innovation is not simply the tail of the dog, it's the whole damn poodle.

CHAPTER 3

How Innovation Matters

The difference between exuberant and cautious growth is not simply that one is faster than the other. Exuberant growth transforms the entire economy. In terms of the critical economic variables–wages, jobs, international competitiveness–the evidence is compelling that innovation-driven economies come out way ahead.

Technological change also brings an excitement and wonder to our daily lives. The ability to travel to distant places, to communicate instantly with people in other parts of the country, to have online access to a vast array of information–all of these capabilities open up new possibilities that capture our attention. In the absence of change, economies are not just slow-growing, they are boring and ultimately failures.

PATHWAYS OF CHANGE

There are three main pathways through which innovation drives growth: the "ramp-up," the "spin-off," and the "free lunch."

Ramp-up: When the innovation first hits the market, and the demand grows very rapidly, there's typically a lot of investment in the new industry and new products. This can give a very big one-time pop to growth. That's what happened in the 1990s, when the advent of the Internet helped propel an enormous amount of investment in information technology and telecom companies and products.

Spin-off: As the innovation takes hold, it transforms other parts of the economy. In some cases–such as information technology and electricity–the effect is to increase the productivity of other industries. But that's not necessarily the only big impact. The automobile, for example, opened up new possibilities for spatial arrangements of work and living, creating the modern suburbs, and transforming the housing market.

Free lunch: Economists like to quote an old saying: "There's no such thing as a free lunch." The idea is that you usually only get what you pay for. In particular, future growth must be paid for by deferring current consumption, and putting it into savings and investment. But big technological breakthroughs violate the free-lunch principle, giving a boost to growth and living standards that goes far beyond any added investment.

Let's look at each of these in turn.

THE RAMP-UP

Almost every new innovation goes through three phases. When initially introduced into the market, the process of adoption is slow. The early models are expensive and hard to use, and perhaps even unsafe. The economic impact is relatively small.

The second phase is the explosive one, where the innovation is rapidly adopted by a large number of people. It gets cheaper and easier to use and becomes something familiar. And then in the third stage, diffusion of the innovation slows down again, as it permeates out across the economy. (This process is also known as the S-curve.)

During the explosive or ramp-up phase, whole new industries spring up to produce the new product or innovation, and to service it. For example, during the 1920s, there was a dramatic acceleration in auto production, from 1.9 million in 1920 to 4.5 million in 1929. This boom was accompanied by all sorts of other essential activities necessary for an auto-based nation: Roads had to be built for the cars to run on; refineries and oil wells, to provide the gasoline; auto dealerships, to sell the cars; and garages, to repair them.

Historically, the same pattern is repeated again and again with innovations. The construction of the electrical system required an enormous early investment in generation and distribution capacity. The introduction of the radio was followed by a buying spree by Americans that quickly brought radios into almost half of all households by 1930, up from nearly none in 1924.

During the 1990s, the arrival of the Internet ignited an even more impressive expansion in the info tech and telecom industries. Purchases of computers, routers, and cabling soared. Employment at software publishers and information technology consultants doubled, and then doubled again. A whole new category of retail computer stores exploded, flourished, and consolidated, leaving behind only a couple of survivors.

The ramp-up effect is like a shot of adrenaline to an economy. It pushes growth much faster than it would otherwise go. By how much? During the tech boom of the 1990s, from 1995 to 2000, business spending on information technology rose at a 21 percent annual rate (adjusted for inflation and increases in computing power), while consumer spending on computers and peripherals rose at an almost 60 percent annual rate (also adjusted for inflation and increases in computing power). Over the same period, the rest of the economy grew at only a 3.1 percent rate. To put that in perspective, that's below the average growth rate for the whole economy in the 1980s. Without the ramp-up effect, the New Economy boom would have been merely a little firecracker.

Looking forward, there are some incipient innovations that could potentially produce a very large ramp-up effect. For example, a widespread shift to the use of hydrogen as a fuel, especially in automobiles, would cost hundreds of billions to retool the energy distribution system. Hydrogen requires a very different infrastructure for storing and delivering than does gasoline. Buried gasoline tanks might be replaced by hydrogen "sponges"–solid materials that store hydrogen. Depending on how fast the shift took place, it could give a nice little boost to growth.

The ramp-up effect is usually ignored by economists, because it is only a one-time bump. Yet it is quite important, especially for the big innovations. The Western world has gone through several periods when innovation followed innovation in rapid succession. If each one gives the economy a little (or a big) jolt, that's enough to keep things moving forward.

THE SPIN-OFF

Any innovation pushes the production capabilities of an economy into new territory. But just as the discovery of a new continent doesn't tell you who will settle it or what kind of nation will evolve there, it's equally hard to predict what kind of impact a new innovation will have. The one that everyone thinks of first is increased labor productivity. However, labor productivity is not the only possible spin-off effect, and for many innovations may not be the most important one.

History suggests that the spin-off effects may take years or even decades to fully manifest themselves. Electricity was introduced toward the end of the 1880s, as Thomas Edison and George Westinghouse waged a great battle to determine whether the electrical system would run on direct current, as Edison proposed, or alternating, as Westinghouse wanted. The unprecedented use of electricity to light the 1893 World's Fair in Chicago was a marvel at the time. As Jill Jonnes wrote in her 2003 book, *Empires of Light*, the Ferris wheel

> glittered in the sky, its gradual (electrically powered)
> turning outlined with three thousand light bulbs. . . .
> The White City illuminated at night was a radiant
> electrical vision long remembered by all who witnessed it.

Nevertheless, several economic studies have shown that it wasn't until the 1920s and 1930s that the use of electricity was widespread enough to boost labor productivity in the U.S., Britain, and Japan.

Similarly, it seems likely that increasingly widespread use of the Internet and Web-enabled businesses is a critical reason why productivity rose so fast in 2002 and 2003. A recent study from the Brookings Institution suggested that the Internet could boost productivity—and overall growth—by up to an extra half percentage point a year.

Innovations may also have a geographical impact that doesn't directly show up in the growth statistics. Before the introduction of the auto, suburbs were located mostly on train lines, with the jobs still in the center cities. But once automobiles became common in the 1920s, it was much easier to live anywhere, or to locate businesses and stores outside of the urban core.

On a slightly less cosmic note, the introduction and spread of air-conditioning is clearly connected with the rise of the Sun Belt states. Once again, there was a time lag between the original invention and the wider impacts. Willis Carrier received the first patent for air-conditioning in 1906, and formed the Carrier Engineering Corporation in 1915. Department stores began being air-conditioned in 1924, and home air-conditioning units followed soon afterward.

Not coincidentally, that marks the moment when the southern region of the country began to take off. Before air-conditioning became commonplace, in the first three decades of the 20th century the South's share of the country's population fell, as farmworkers headed north to the booming factories. Georgia actually lost population in the 1920s. But as air-conditioning made living and working in the South more attractive, growth picked up and hasn't yet stopped. (The ramifications of air-conditioning still persist today, making tropical and subtropical countries reasonable places to relocate factories.)

Innovations in health, especially for the elderly, are a boon for longevity and quality of life, but don't necessarily show up in the official economic statistics. GDP—gross domestic product—measures production, as the name implies. Imagine that the biotech revolution starts paying off, in terms of effective cures for major diseases. Longevity would rise significantly, but perhaps at a very large cost. There's no doubt that many people would find it worthwhile to divert money from other things—such as housing—to pay for more years of life. However—and this is a big however—

those extra years of life would have almost no direct impact on growth, especially if the prime beneficiaries are older people who have already left the workforce.

In a less serious context, another example of a spin-off effect is Internet dating. The drive to meet a mate and start a family is one of the most powerful that we have. The widespread use of Internet personal ad sites dramatically increases the pool of potential partners, drawing from a wider range of geographical locations. Even within a local area, we are no longer bound by our friends and work partners—the search can reach out and touch many different subgroups of society.

The larger implications of Internet dating are not yet clear. In theory, access to more potential partners will improve the quality of matches, which should lead to fewer divorces. At the same time, Internet dating should lead to more cross-country or cross-border relationships, which may be harder to sustain.

Or consider the field of entertainment, where video and computer games comprise a whole new mode of amusement that did not exist before. We can be more or less skeptical of the intellectual or moral value of such best-selling games as Grand Theft Auto: Vice City, but their appeal cannot be denied (especially to certain age classes). Amusement is an important human need, which is not generally captured by purely economic variables.

THE "FREE LUNCH"

One of the surprising things about innovation is that it emphatically breaks the link between savings and growth. A country or a company that makes better use of a new technology can potentially leap far ahead of one that saves and invests more. Innovation is, as was said above, the economic equivalent of a free lunch.

In some sense, this goes against the values drilled into us when we are young. Traditionally we respect people–and countries–who save more. Putting money away for the future and then reaping the benefits later on seems like an admirable thing to do, even if we don't save ourselves.

In particular, in the 1980s, Japan, with a national savings rate in excess of 30 percent of GDP, was held up as a paragon of virtue. (National savings is computed by combining the savings of households and corporations, while subtracting the budget deficit of the government.) Meanwhile the U.S. with a national savings rate that only averaged 16 percent of GDP, developed a reputation, both domestically and globally, as a myopic, consumerist culture. Especially during Japan's boom years of the late 1980s, Japanese prime ministers would lecture the U.S. on the need to increase the savings rate. *Fortune* magazine wrote in 1988:

> Since at least the Book of Proverbs–"A wise man saves for the future, but a foolish man spends whatever he gets"–saving has stood as a test of virtue. America looks to be flunking the test these days. . . . Moral fiber aside, persistent undersaving is a ticket to economic oblivion if a nation cannot invest in tomorrow's productive machinery and individuals cannot be sure of a good future.

The same year, Senator Lloyd Bentsen, a Democrat and later treasury secretary in President Bill Clinton's first term, called the savings rate "a disgrace." In 1989, both Democrats and Republicans on the Joint Economic Committee of Congress agreed that the nation's chief economic problem was a low savings rate.

But it turned out that having a high savings rate did not prevent Japan from its slowdown in the 1990s, and having a low savings rate did not stop the U.S. from having a boom in the 1990s. In fact, despite being mired in a long slump, Japan still had much higher savings and investment rates than the U.S. throughout the decade. From 1995 to 2000, the national savings rate in Japan averaged 29 percent of GDP, compared with 18 percent in the U.S. That's a slightly smaller gap than in the 1980s, but there's no doubt that the Japanese were still better savers than the Americans, even during the New Economy boom years.

The free-lunch effect was stronger than the "virtue" of savings and investment. The U.S. leapt ahead because American companies and individuals were better able to apply the new innovations and ideas of the Information Revolution. In the end, bright ideas, risk-taking, and execution were more important than how much money we saved and invested.

BIGGER WAGE GAINS

In the short run, it's possible or even likely that some workers may be hurt by technological change, if their jobs are eliminated or transformed. There is, however, little reason to doubt that the best way to raise the wages of the poor and the working class is to encourage rapid exuberant growth. In *The Wealth of Nations*, Adam Smith said it as clearly as possible:

> Though the wealth of a country should be very great, yet if it has been long stationary, we must not expect to find the wages of labour very high in it.

Over the long term, wages basically rise parallel with productivity. True, there is usually a bit of a lag between changes in productivity growth and changes in wage growth. When productivity accelerated in the exuberant growth period of the second half of the 1990s, it took a couple of years before those gains showed up in higher wages. Eventually, though, they did, and real earnings of virtually all workers soared. From 1993 to 2003, real wages for all workers, adjusted for inflation, rose by 9 percent, based on wage and price data from the Bureau of Labor Statistics. That's outstanding, especially when compared with a gain of only 1 percent from 1983 to 1993, the previous 10-year period.

It wasn't just the well-to-do and educated who benefited. Real hourly earnings for production and nonsupervisory workers rose by 8 percent. The percentage of families living below the poverty line fell sharply, from 12.3 percent in 1993 to 9.6 percent in 2002, the last year available. By comparison, the poverty rate was flat in the stretch from 1983 to 1993. Even the 2001 recession and subsequent slow downturn seems to have eroded only part of the gains. By contrast, the periods when cautious growth has dominated have typically had very slow wage growth, adjusted for inflation, especially for the people at the bottom.

For the most part, the historical record suggests that periods of innovation have generally been a good thing for the working class. For example, the question of what happened to workers during the rapid technological change of the British Industrial Revolution of the 19th century has been hotly debated. Nevertheless, from 1810 to 1850, argued Jeffrey Williamson, a Harvard economic historian, "blue-collar workers' real wages doubled." Williamson also estimated that the percentage of paupers in the population—the extreme poor—dropped from 15 percent in 1812 down to 10 percent in 1850 and 6.2 percent in 1867.

In the 20th century, it was the leading-edge industries such as automobile manufacturing that were able to afford to pay the best wages. It was automobile pioneer Henry Ford who boosted his factory's daily wage to $5.00 a day in 1914, when the going wage for factory workers was less than $2.50 per day. More recently, workers in the tech sector enjoyed some of the biggest wage gains in the 1990s.

The right way to think about it is that innovation generates a surplus–the free lunch–which goes to workers, in the form of higher wages, and to companies, in the form of higher profits. It's often a nasty battle over how the free lunch will be split. But if the surplus doesn't exist, there's nothing to fight over.

MORE JOBS

Both logic and history suggest that it's far easier to generate high-paying, attractive new jobs in an exuberant economy, compared with a cautious one. Typically big technological breakthroughs create new and profitable industries, which need a lot of workers and are willing to pay good money.

It's possible to go down the list of industries published by the BLS and identify what innovations in the past led to which jobs. Today there are perhaps 9 million workers employed making motor vehicles and airplanes, selling them, servicing them, or working in closely connected industries. Another 4 million are directly engaged in making high-tech equipment, selling it, or helping people deal with it. Another 1 million work in the electric utility industry, or building electrical equipment. Another 1.5 million or so work in the telephone, radio, and television industries.

Then, of course, there are the indirect jobs that are spun off from the original innovations. Virtually the entire travel industry depends on the availability of cheap air and land travel. Destinations such as Disney World would not be economically viable if their customers could only come from the surrounding areas.

Similarly, the retail and wholesale industries are absolutely dependent in their current form on the truck/air/rail distribution system. Wal-Mart, the largest private employer in the country, built its business model around effective use of information technology and far-flung sourcing of cheap products. And while it's not possible to separate out the effects of medical innovation on health care employment, there's no doubt that there would be far less money spent on health care, and far fewer health care jobs, if it wasn't for all the new treatments introduced over the last 50 years.

Interestingly enough, periods of innovation and exuberant growth also seem to be the periods of the lowest unemployment and the fastest job growth. In the 1960s, when productivity was growing very quickly, unemployment dropped below 4 percent. As innovation and productivity growth slowed in the 1970s and 1980s, unemployment rose. And then, as the economy went through another innovation and productivity spurt in the 1990s, unemployment dropped below 4 percent again.

Why should this be? During periods of cautious growth, companies have only one way to boost productivity and profits—by cutting costs and trimming the ranks of workers. These surplus workers are left unemployed, or they may move into the service sector—the dry-cleaning, health care, restaurant, retailing, and other service jobs that grow almost every year, along with the population. The problem is that these jobs don't necessarily pay well. Restaurants always need waiters and waitresses, but that doesn't mean that they can afford to pay a good wage.

However, during periods of exuberant growth, both companies and workers have other options. Innovation enables companies to compete—not necessarily by cutting labor, but by using new technology to make existing workers more productive. And when workers are laid off, there are innovative new industries that are hiring.

In an exuberant economy, workers have something to aspire to–there's unclaimed territory where smart and hardworking Americans can make their mark. Without innovation, the job market congeals and stagnates. There is no way for anyone to move up without bumping someone else down.

EASIER RETIREMENT

Exuberant growth is absolutely essential for dealing with the biggest economic problem that we face today: the looming task of financing the retirement of the baby boom generation. There are lots of different parts to this puzzle–the rising number of retirees compared with working people, the soaring costs of health care, the need to find resources for long-term care–but they all come down to the same thing. The economy has to grow–a lot–over the next 20 years to pay for all the obligations, and cautious growth simply won't be sufficient to make the economic pie big enough for everyone. Exuberant growth, however, makes the retirement problem tractable, as the appendix to this chapter shows.

IMPROVED COMPETITIVENESS

Equally important, exuberant growth is the only way that a mature industrial economy such as the U.S. can compete against low-cost competitors overseas. If the U.S. is not extending its technological lead, it becomes much easier for other countries to catch up.

For example, it was during the 20-year period of cautious growth, from 1973 to the mid-1990s, that the U.S. lost much of its international competitiveness, the U.S. trade deficit exploded, and manufacturers moved jobs out of the country.

During this period, the U.S. seemed helpless to hold back the tide of imports from overseas. Cautious growth depends on investment in physical capital, and that's not one of America's strong points. Other countries have much higher savings rates, as well as less expensive workers. There was no way for the U.S. to compete on those terms.

Exuberant growth, instead, builds on the real competitive advantage that the U.S. has–not in capital, not in education, but in risk-taking. Other countries simply don't have the resources to take a chance on an expensive new technology the way that the U.S. does. At the same time, exuberant growth in the U.S. turns out to be enormously beneficial to other countries as well. Think of the process of economic development as a ladder. The bottom rung is agriculture and natural resources. The next rung up is light manufacturing, such as textiles and clothing. Then comes heavier industrial processes such as steel making, followed by more advanced industrial production such as automobiles, which is in turn followed by high-tech products such as electronics.

It is only natural for successful countries to keep moving up the ladder. That's what happened with Japan, Korea, and Taiwan, and that's what is happening now with China and India. As countries develop, their industrial capabilities increase, and so does the range of products that they can make.

Exuberant growth has the effect of allowing the U.S. to keep moving to higher and higher rungs on the ladder. Technological change creates new products and new markets that can be exploited for a time, before other countries catch up. In the 1990s it was high tech, software, the Internet, and biotech leading the way.

And as the U.S. and other advanced countries move on to new markets, it opens up the lower rungs of the ladder for other nations. Taiwan and Korea can move up to producing electronics components and even whole computers for the U.S., while China can produce the toys and other products that were once "Made in Taiwan." India can attract call centers and help desks–routine and repetitive tasks that can easily be outsourced.

HIGHER PURPOSES

We can't simply compare exuberant and cautious growth based on economic considerations. No matter what is taught in Econ 101, most people are not motivated purely by pecuniary motives or by self-interest (with the notable exception of some Gordon Gecko "greed is good" types who may be found on Wall Street or in Silicon Valley). There has to be an emotional component, to keep us going, and a higher purpose, to satisfy our souls.

What the best innovations do is create new possibilities that didn't exist before. The airplane opened up entirely new avenues for travel and trade. The radio created new possibilities for entertainment and communication. The result of innovation is not just economic growth, but growth of the human spirit as well. It reinforces curiosity and risk-taking, and the idea that there is always something new behind the next mountain.

The Internet boom, along with a soaring stock market, provided both a positive emotional component and at least the hint of a higher purpose. People enjoyed what they were doing, for the most part, and they felt like they were making a difference. In the words of one *Wall Street Journal* columnist, recalling the 1990s wistfully, it was "the pure, simple, social fun of a real economy– teams of people dreaming up ways to do things that have never been done before."

Silicon Valley was attractive both because people were making big money and because there seemed to be an opportunity to make a difference. Bringing the Internet to people became something of a crusade, and the people working in these companies felt like missionaries. Following the example of Apple Computer, Netscape and other leading Internet companies had employees who held a job with the official or unofficial title of "Evangelist" to spread the gospel of the Internet–something that would not have occurred with a steel company or a car company.

Exuberant growth *feels* vibrant. Like hitting a rich vein of ore or sexual attraction, exuberant growth is what provides the excitement and the verve in mature economies. New opportunities open up to succeed–and to fail.

Moreover, innovation gives a sense of progress, that things will be better for our children and our children's children. That's essential–it provides a motivation for people that goes beyond the economic. It gives us a reason to wake up and go to work in the morning, if we believe that our efforts will make things better for other people.

Without innovation, the status quo solidifies. If the underlying technologies don't change, then the corporate and job structure don't change either. That makes it much harder for people on the bottom and for young workers to move up. Change and ferment provide an opening and an opportunity, give purpose to the people just starting out, and provide them with a reason to participate.

APPENDIX TO CHAPTER 3:
THE ARITHMETIC OF BABY BOOMER RETIREMENT

There's tremendous debate about the possibility of a demographic calamity in the U.S. when the baby boomer generation retires.

However, the arithmetic of retirement changes dramatically depending on whether the U.S. experiences cautious or exuberant growth over the next three decades. Here are the simple demographic facts first. Over the next 30 years, according to the U.S. Census Bureau, the population in the U.S. will increase by roughly 27 percent. But the prime-age working population, ages 25–64, will increase only 12 percent. That means each worker has to become 13 percent more productive just to maintain a constant per-person income for everyone—workers, retirees, children (see Table 2 for calculations).

Historical patterns indicate that a cautious-growth economy will generate productivity growth of only 1.1 percent per year, or only a 39 percent increase for the whole 30-year period. If 13 percent is already committed to compensate for the increase in the non-working population, that doesn't leave much for everyone and everything else.

In this scenario, per-person income would only rise at an annual rate of 0.7 percent over the next 30 years. That's compared to the long-term average annual gain of 2.1 percent. With cautious growth, the demographic drag would absorb a large portion of the productivity gains. The children of the middle class would do no better than their parents. And the generational wars would be horrendous.

These are the simple facts for an economy with cautious growth. No matter what kind of fancy private or public financing we whip up for Social Security, no matter how we try to reform the medical care system—with a single payer model or complete privatization—it's a recipe for political and technological disaster. There simply aren't enough resources.

By contrast, exuberant growth, powered by technological changes, makes the interlocked problems much more manageable. Over the 30-year period, productivity per worker goes up by about 92 percent. It then becomes possible to pay for the baby boomer retirement and rising medical costs, and still have plenty left over.

TABLE 2: TWO SCENARIOS FOR THE NEXT 30 YEARS		
	PERCENTAGE INCREASE, 2005–2035	
	CAUTIOUS GROWTH	EXUBERANT GROWTH
Total population	27	27
Prime-age working population	12	12
Rise in productivity needed to keep per-person income constant	13	13
Total rise in productivity	39	92
Amount available for higher per-person income	23	71
Annual increase in per-person income	**0.7**	**1.8**

CHAPTER 4

The Economic Enemies of Growth

Exuberant growth has enemies. So does innovation. It is incontrovertible that technological change has been the prime mover for economic growth over the last 100 years. Nevertheless, there are broad swaths of the educated class who find innovation-driven growth to be unnatural, at best, and destructive, at worst.

In particular, the very group that one might hope would be the advocate of technology-driven growth—the economics profession—has by and large turned out to be its enemy. In textbooks and in policy pronouncements, some of the best-known and most influential members of the profession have over the years consistently ignored or belittled technology. At the same time, they promoted policies that by their own calculations would give only a minimal lift to long-term growth.

This is not meant to tar all economists with the same brush.

The strong productivity performance of recent years has meant that even skeptics acknowledge the importance of information technology. Moreover, there are some who have enthusiastically embraced the idea that encouraging innovation and technological change is the best way to boost growth. In particular, that's the message of New Growth Theory, originally proposed by Paul Romer of Stanford University in the 1980s.

But there's an incontrovertible fact: By systematically underplaying the role of technology and innovation to students and to policymakers, economists have seriously undercut the support for exuberant growth, whether they meant to or not.

THE DISMAL SCIENCE

When we look at the opponents of exuberant growth, the right place to start is with the economists. We would expect that if the notably fractious economics profession agreed on anything, it would be that growth is good.

But the truth is very different. The central tradition of the economics profession is profoundly ambivalent about technology. Its importance is acknowledged, but most economists are naturally pessimistic, with a strong preference for prudent and cautious growth.

Even today, most economists are what has been called "capital fundamentalists"–true believers in the primacy of tangible investment, both physical and human. In the conventional view, the way to improve long-term growth is by increasing savings and investment first, and by raising education and training levels second. Doing anything to encourage technological change, if the topic comes up at all, is given only perfunctory attention.

The lack of faith in "technological progress" is deeply embedded in the economics profession, going back to the Reverend Thomas Malthus, who published his famous book *An Essay on the Principle of Population* in 1798, when the Industrial Revolution was well under way. In the first edition of his essay, Malthus framed the division between the technological optimists and technological pessimists in this way:

> The great question is now at issue, whether man shall henceforth start forwards with accelerated velocity towards illimitable; and hitherto unconceived improvement, or be condemned to a perpetual oscillation between happiness and misery, and after every effort remain still at an immeasurable distance from the wished-for goal.

His conclusion, of course, was that population growth was bound to outstrip any possible gains in food production. And thus, he denied the possibility of a society in which

> all the members of which should live in ease, happiness, and comparative leisure; and feel no anxiety about providing the means of subsistence for themselves and families.

This profoundly pessimistic strain of economics was moderated by the Industrial Revolution of the 19th century, which did see real incomes rising in Britain and the U.S., and advances in agriculture and food production keeping well ahead of population growth.

By the end of the 1800s, economists were willing to grant technological advance at least a place at the table. Alfred Marshall, the British economist who was one of the cofounders of modern economics, wrote in his 1890s classic, *Principles of Economics,* that "knowledge is our most powerful engine of production." Indeed, the explosive growth of the early 1900s, through the 1920s, seemed inextricably tied to new technologies such as autos and electricity.

Still, technology was not one of the central concerns of economics. Certainly there were some economists in the early 20th century, such as Joseph Schumpeter, who wrote about innovation. Nevertheless, a 2002 book on the history of economics observes that "such ideas . . . can be regarded as marginal to the pure theory that was becoming increasingly prominent."

The Great Depression reinforced the natural pessimism of economists. Their belief, and the belief of many Americans, was that technology, by boosting farm and factory productivity, was creating massive and intractable unemployment. That made technology part of the cause of the deep downturn, rather than part of the solution.

Most economists did not expect a new round of technological progress to bail out the country. In his 1938 presidential address to the American Economics Association, Alvin Hansen, perhaps the leading Keynesian economist in the U.S., explained that

> when giant new industries have spent their force, it may
> take a long time before something else of equal magnitude
> emerges.

The result, he said, is "secular stagnation":

> sick recoveries which die in their infancy and depressions
> which feed on themselves and leave a hard and seemingly
> immovable core of unemployment.

To combat this problem, the key insight of Keynesian economics was that the U.S. and Europe were suffering from insufficient demand, which could be solved by more government spending. That would become the core of economic policy making, with technology taking a deep second place. After all, technology advances don't matter much if unemployment is 25 percent.

THE SOLOW DIVERGENCE

Technology reappeared in economics in the late 1950s, when Robert Solow published his papers on growth theory, which eventually won him the Nobel Prize in Economics. As mentioned in Chapter 2, his results suggested, quite strongly, that technological change played a key role in propelling long-term growth. Although disputed by some, the Solow results were so compelling that they were accepted by most of the economics profession relatively quickly. They provided a genuine insight into the way that the world works, and remain one of the few economic results that have stood the test of time.

However, the reaction of the economics profession to the Solow papers was surprising. Rather than paying more attention to technology and innovation, the economics community relegated technological change to the role of the dotty old aunt living in the attic. Economists acknowledged its existence, but preferred instead to focus on physical and human capital accumulation, something that they understood much better.

To put it another way, imagine that growth is like a cherry pie, where technology is the filling and capital investment is the crust. What the economics profession did was specialize in making the crust—an essential part of the pie, of course, but not the tastiest and most nutritious part.

We can only speculate why, for 30 years, economists turned away from technology. One reason could be that most economists are simply not comfortable with technology—they learned about supply and demand, not semiconductors, in school. Equally important, technological innovation is an essentially unpredictable process, which cannot be reduced to the equations preferred by economists. That made it simply easier to ignore.

ERRORS OF OMISSION

Many economists might object vociferously at this point, saying that the economics profession certainly does take technology seriously. After all, there are academics who specialize in the economics of innovation and R&D, and Solow received the Nobel Prize in Economics for his work on economic growth and technology. And they will certainly assure you in private that technology is very important.

Yet based on the public face, technology is still at best a minor area of economics. For example, at the annual meeting of the American Economics Association in January 2004, only 9 out of 130 sessions had any substantial papers on the economic impact of technology (omitting sessions on using computer technology to teach economics).

A particularly striking fact is that it's entirely possible to write a history of the economics profession with barely any mention of technological change. *Lost Prophets,* a 1994 book covering the leading postwar economists by a *Wall Street Journal* economics writer, makes only the briefest mention of technology. Similarly, there are no references to technology or innovation in a more recent book on the history of economics, entitled *A Perilous Progress: Economists and Public Purpose in 20th Century America,* published in 2001.

The extent to which top economists have avoided dealing with technology is surprising. Take, for example, Milton Friedman, the University of Chicago economist. A hero to conservatives and winner of the Nobel Prize in Economics in 1976, Friedman has written two of the classic defenses of capitalism, his 1962 book, *Capitalism and Freedom,* and the 1980 bestseller *Free to Choose,* written with his wife, Rose Friedman.

One might think that technological progress would be cited as one of the main advantages of capitalism, since no other economic system has been able to match its track record. But the words "technology" and "innovation" do not appear in the index of the 1980 book, and science gets only a brief mention. Similarly, science and technology take distinctly minor billing in his 1962 classic. At one point, Friedman does briefly mention "the opportunities offered by modern science and technology," but later in the book he shows his basic disdain toward organized science, writing:

> Advances in any science or field often result from the work
> of one out of a large number of crackpots and quacks and
> people who have no standing in the profession.

Or consider the book *American Economic Policy in the 1980s,* a comprehensive 800-page collection of papers on that decade, put out in 1994 by the National Bureau of Economic Research. Reading this volume, one finds only glancing references to technology and innovation (which do not appear in the index at all). There is a section on the telecommunications industry, but focused mainly on the regulatory aspect rather than technology.

That omission includes the lead essay, written by Martin Feldstein, clearly one of today's preeminent economists—professor of economics at Harvard University, president of the National Bureau of Economic Research, head of the Council of Economic Advisers under Ronald Reagan, and winner of the 1977 John Bates

Clark Award (given to the most outstanding economist under the age of 40). "The ability to raise our national savings rate will be an important determinant of our economic success in the 1990s and beyond," wrote Feldstein. Any mention of technology or innovation? None.

The liberal side of the economics profession has been equally guilty of pretending technology doesn't exist. In 1997, the Brookings Institution, the top liberal economic think tank, laid out its policy agenda for Clinton's second term in office in a book entitled *Setting National Priorities*. One of the main purposes of the book was proposing policy prescriptions for increasing the nation's growth rate, such as cutting the budget deficit and other Washington-oriented policy measures. What's astonishing is that even as the Internet was gaining momentum, there was no mention of technology at all.

BELITTLING TECHNOLOGY

When it proved impossible to ignore technology in the middle of the 1990s, economists switched to belittling it, and trying to minimize its impact. Despite the rise of personal computers and the Internet, many of the most prominent economic experts treated the very notion of a tech-driven productivity boom with disdain. Alan Blinder–a Princeton economist, former member of Clinton's Council of Economic Advisers, and former vice chairman of the Federal Reserve–wrote in *The American Prospect* in 1997:

> Mainstream economists are exceptionally united right now
> around the proposition that the trend growth rate of real
> gross domestic product (GDP) in the United States . . . is in
> the 2 percent to 2.5 percent range. . . . Nothing–I repeat,
> nothing–economists know about growth gives us a recipe

for adding a percentage point or more to the nation's
growth rate on a sustained basis.

Perhaps the two most aggressive belittlers of technology in the
1990s were also two of the most prominent economists, Paul Krugman and N. Gregory Mankiw. Krugman–professor of economics at
Princeton, also a winner of the John Bates Clark Award (in 1991),
and best-selling columnist for the *New York Times*–has spent much
of the last decade repeatedly denigrating the economic impact of
technology. The attacks started well before the New Economy was
even a glimmer in anyone's mind. In 1991, Krugman wrote:

> High technology is fashionable, and I think we are all
> obliged to make a deliberate effort to fight against
> fashionable ideas. It is all too easy to fall into a kind of facile
> "megatrends" style of thought in which the wonders of the
> new are cited and easy assumptions are made that
> everything is different now.

In the following years, Krugman came back to the same point,
over and over, repeatedly expressing his disdain for technology.
For example, in June 1998, he wrote an article in *Red Herring* magazine, in which he stated: "The truth is that we live in an age not of
extraordinary progress but of technological disappointment. And
that's why the future is not what it used to be." In 1999, he deni-
grated the impact of the space program, writing in *Fortune* that "30
years after the moon landings, we now know it was one small step
for man, one expensive photo op for mankind." And in 2000, he
came back to the same theme again, writing that:

> technology is not a magic elixir. The Internet, mobile
> phones and all that are exciting and important, but those

who count on them to solve all their problems are likely to be disappointed.

If Krugman was dismissive of technology from the liberal side of the spectrum, equal scorn came from the conservative side, in the person of N. Gregory Mankiw—a Harvard professor acclaimed as one of the best economists of his generation, author of a bestselling textbook, and chairman of the Council of Economic Advisers under George W. Bush. In 1995, Mankiw published a paper entitled "The Growth of Nations," in which he effectively called technological progress a question too insignificant for economists to even bother thinking about.

> In my view, however, the goal is not to explain the *existence* of economic growth. That task is too easy: it is obvious that living standards rise over time largely because knowledge expands and production functions improve. [Emphasis in original]

The same attitude toward technology shows up loud and clear in Mankiw's *Principles of Macroeconomics* textbook, often described as the successor to Paul Samuelson's classic text. The student reading the textbook is left with a clear idea of the unimportance of technology. Technology gets only the briefest of mentions in the introduction, where the main themes of the textbook are laid out. Then, when it makes a short appearance in the discussion of supply and demand, it's trivialized as "the invention of the mechanized ice cream machine."

When Mankiw returns to the subject of technological knowledge again, he lists it as only the fourth factor contributing to productivity, after physical capital, human capital, and natural resources. Similarly, spending on research and development is put last in a long list of government policies for boosting productivity. He then doesn't come back to the importance of technology to growth until page 440 of a 540-page textbook. And as any student knows, the stuff that is at the end of a textbook is there for a reason–the author considers it less important.

Being pessimistic about technology, Mankiw is willing to accept the slow pace of growth during the 1970s and 1980s as the norm:

> What does the future hold for technological progress and economic growth? . . . History can, however, give us a sense of what is the normal rate of technological progress. . . . Perhaps the decades after World War II were a period of unusually rapid technological advance, and growth slowed down in 1973 simply because technological progress was returning to a more normal rate.

He still held the same skeptical views about productivity in 2002, when he wrote the opening essay for a 1,000-page book entitled *American Economic Policy in the 1990s.* Mankiw's take on the 1990s is simple.

> During these years there was much discussion of the "new economy" and the increasing role of information technology. . . . While the productivity speed-up is a fortuitous development, its importance should not be overstated. Compared to the data from the 1950s and the 1960s, the average rate of productivity growth during the 1990s is not unusual.

Mankiw's standoffish attitude toward technology persisted even after he became head of the Council of Economic Advisers. In a September 2003 speech, he continued to argue that "the sources of strong productivity growth are hard to identify." The speech contains no mention of the economic benefits of computers or the Internet, but the ice cream machine–the same one as in his textbook, presumably–makes several appearances.

POST-BOOM ECONOMICS

As this book is being written, the U.S. has turned in eight years of exceptional productivity growth. Thus, with a few notable exceptions, even many economists who formerly ignored or dismissed technology have been forced to give it a more prominent role in their analysis of the economy. For example, Feldstein, in a paper presented at the 2003 annual meeting of the American Economics Association, wrote that "the use of the internet and corporate intranets not only makes individuals more productive as they search and process information but also permits significant reductions in staff levels." This paper represented an important shift by a very important economist. Blinder, too, has been willing to give more emphasis to the influence of technology on productivity growth.

Nevertheless, their embrace of technology has not been wholehearted. For example, in the same paper Feldstein writes, "even if the technical changes in information technology had not occurred, the pressures to raise profits and reduce costs would have led to a greater increase in productivity in the U.S." Such statements downplay the role of technology in growth.

Moreover, the disdain toward technology still shows up in many if not most economics textbooks. The treatment of technology in Mankiw's textbook has already been mentioned. Similarly, in the 2003 edition of their best-selling principles textbook, Blinder and his coauthor William Baumol (a famous economist in his own right) make a big deal about how "Productivity Growth Is (Almost) Everything in the Long Run." However, they manage to discuss the benefits of rising productivity without mentioning its connection with technology.

Then, when they finally get to their chapter on growth, they still manage to convey their suspicion of technological innovation very clearly to the student. Right at the beginning of the chapter, they poke fun at "naive observers" who believed in an "economy of abundance" and "the super-optimists" who "imagined a world in which ever-growing productivity would lead to ever-growing incomes and ever-growing consumer demand."

Baumol and Blinder actually say straight out that the U.S. should not try to speed up innovation by spending more on R&D.

> The notion that we are spending far too small a share of GDP on innovation is not really very plausible. Looking about us, we see a flood of new products and processes, but certainly nothing that suggests a dearth of new technology.

Earlier textbooks were more likely to just treat technology in a perfunctory manner rather than with disdain. Take Paul Samuelson's *Economics,* for decades the leader in the field. Picking an edition at random (the 11th edition published in 1980), it starts out a bit better than other textbooks. Early in the book, Samuelson concedes that "technical invention may more than match productivity gain from thrift alone." As a result, "Economy B, blessed by scientific and engineering discoveries, might surpass thriftier A, which was investing more for the future but with less progressive technology." But after that good start, the next significant mention of innovation doesn't come until page 685.

Does the offhand and minimal treatment of technology in Mankiw, Samuelson, and other textbooks matter? As Samuelson said, "I don't care who writes a nation's laws–or crafts its advanced treaties–if I can write its economics textbooks." Even today, Econ 101 students are getting a clear signal that technology is not important to the economy–and that's not a good thing.

ECONOMIC POLICY WITHOUT TECHNOLOGY

Once economists have ignored or dismissed technology, then the only way to boost growth is to accumulate physical and human capital. In other words, the path to virtue and success is to increase savings and investment, cut budget deficits and consumption, and in general build up our stock of useful buildings, machines, and skills.

Such capital fundamentalism was and still is almost inescapable in the Washington policy debate. This prescription is the core of what's known as the "Washington Consensus," advocated by many mainstream economists, built into the charter of the European Union, and embodied in the advice that the International Monetary Fund gives to developing countries, and for that matter, to industrialized countries as well. In a March 2003 speech, the managing director of the International Monetary Fund, Horst Kohler, talking about Latin American countries, said that they needed to adopt "a culture of living within one's means."

Not surprisingly, Mankiw is one of the most forthright of capital fundamentalists. Writing in *Fortune* in 1999, Mankiw wrote: "The best case for increased saving, however, is simply that it is the surest way to promote more rapid economic growth." In his textbook, students learn that "countries that devote a large share of

GDP to investment, such as Singapore and Japan, tend to have high growth rates."

Today, it's common for economists to start a textbook or policy piece by admitting that technology is important, and then proceed to ignore it afterward and focus completely on capital accumulation. For example, in fall 2003, in anticipation of the coming presidential election, Brookings published a book entitled *Agenda for the Nation*, which was supposed to lay out policies for the next few years. The economic policy essay starts off by acknowledging that "ideas—and the technology that derives from them—are the primary long-term cause of economic growth." Indeed, one of the essay's authors, J. Bradford DeLong of the University of California at Berkeley, is well-known for his interest in technology. Nevertheless, rather than offering proposals for promoting technology directly, the essay's main policy suggestions were to run a budget surplus and spend more on education and training: "One line of policy, however, is both straightforward and effective in boosting capital accumulation and growth: The government should run a budget surplus."

THE FAILURE OF CAPITAL FUNDAMENTALISM

No one will deny that encouraging savings and investment is a good thing. But here's a secret that economists don't want you to know: In the absence of technological change, even big jumps in savings and investment don't yield much in terms of growth. Or as one authoritative review of the growth literature reported in 1999:

> A consensus has emerged that the correlation between equipment investment and growth appears to be weak in the OECD.

In lay language, that means increases in capital investment by themselves don't add much to growth.

Even economists who are wholehearted capital fundamentalists can only find a small effect of savings and investment on growth. For example, in an article for the 1999 *Handbook of Macroeconomics,* Mankiw and his coauthor Douglas Elmendorf examined what would happen if the "debt fairy" came and took away all U.S. government bonds and gifted the U.S. with the same amount of productive buildings and equipment. Their answer? Economic output would go up by about 5 percent.

That really is a very small gain for such a big change. Consider that eliminating today's $4 trillion in government debt held by the public would require the federal government to run a $200 billion surplus annually for the next 20 years. By comparison, the Internet-led boom helped add an additional 7 percent to GDP in less than a decade.

Most of the economic literature comes to the same conclusion: that increases in investment, in the absence of technological change, doesn't make that much of a difference in boosting growth. For example, in his 1997 book, *Determinants of Economic Growth,* Robert Barro–an economist at Harvard University who is regularly mentioned as a candidate for a Nobel Prize, and a columnist at *BusinessWeek*–discusses at length the impacts of various factors on growth across different countries. When he looks at increases in the ratio of investment to output, holding everything else constant, he concludes that the "positive effect on growth is weak."

Similarly, even large changes in the government budget deficit don't affect growth very much either. Consider the numbers in a January 2004 report from the Brookings Institution entitled "Restoring Fiscal Sanity." The editors of the report–noted economists Alice Rivlin, a former vice chair of the Federal Reserve, and Isabel

Sawhill—indicate their alarm at the government's large budget deficits, arguing that "the nation's fiscal situation is out of control and could do serious damage to the economy in coming decades." The report calculates that "if nothing is done, the national debt is projected to increase by $5.3 trillion in the next decade alone," a horrifying number.

However, the direct economic damage from those big budget deficits turns out to be rather small. Based on the estimates in the Brookings report, the $5 trillion debt buildup would cut a bit more than 1 percent off of GDP by 2014. That translates into reducing the 10-year growth rate by a minuscule 0.1 percentage point—almost a rounding error.

It's also worth noting that large-scale reform of the Social Security system turns out to have little effect on long-term growth. Feldstein, for example, has proposed shifting to a system of "personal retirement accounts" complementing the current Social Security system, funded by deposits equal to 2.3 percent of individual earnings (up to the Social Security earnings limit). That's roughly $100 billion today. The impact, according to Feldstein, would be "an increase in the real rate of growth of about 0.08 per cent per year."

What's the rationale for working so hard for so little gain? Basically, the reason is that economists know how to cut the budget deficit, but they don't understand how to encourage or influence technology. Feldstein wrote, in *American Economic Policy in the 1980s:*

> Although growth theory implied that increased capital accumulation would have only a modest effect on per capita GNP, it was the only determinant of growth that seemed susceptible to changes in economic policy.

The authors of the article in the 2003 Brookings volume used the same reasoning:

> No one yet knows enough to design systems that will successfully nurture investment in ideas and technology.

Thus, the focus on budget deficits, rather than technology, is very much like that old story of the man who lost his contact lens in a dark alley. Instead of looking there, he went to search for it in the street, because "that's where the light is." Seemingly logical, but ultimately not very effective.

A NOTE ON THE INVESTMENT BOOM OF THE 1990S

But wait—didn't the 1990s show how an investment boom can drive growth? The U.S. had plenty of growth, but in retrospect, without much of an investment boom.

Just look at the numbers. From 1995 to 2000, the average share of GDP going to business investment was 11.8 percent. That's not very much higher than the 11.5 percent average of the previous 20 years, from 1975 through 1994. The differential stays the same when we look at net investment, which takes out depreciation. In that case, the share of GDP going to business investment, after deducting depreciation, averaged 3.6 percent in the period from 1995 to 2000, versus 3.3 percent in the previous 20 years.

What happened was that an increase in spending in computers during that period was mostly balanced out by weak spending on other types of equipment and structures. What's more, computers depreciate faster than buildings, which drags down net investment.

UNPREDICTABILITY: THE BANE OF ECONOMICS

Most economic forecasters are enemies of exuberant growth as well. The reason is simple. The elements of cautious growth, investment in physical and human capital, are easy to predict, and factor into their forecasts. But as we will see in Chapter 6, technological innovation is unpredictable, and given to wide and abrupt swings. Thus, it's only natural for forecasters to focus on the part of the economy they understand and can predict–the investment and educational levels–and minimize the importance of technology.

If Solow or one of his successors had discovered that physical and human capital accumulation could explain all or most growth, then economists would be the most respected of social scientists. Their forecasting models would be accurate, rather than being hit-or-miss. Then economic growth would be highly predictable, and economics would be much closer to a true science, like physics or chemistry.

The uncertainty of innovation has been responsible for all of the big forecasting failures of the past. For example, nobody expected the sharp slowdown in productivity growth in the second half of the 1970s and early 1980s. What was the cause? It wasn't low capital investment, since business investment averaged 12.1 percent of GDP in those years, a bit higher than during the boom. And the percentage of Americans with a college degree was rising sharply, as the generation of young people who went to school to avoid the draft was finally graduating. Indeed, as late as January 1977, President Gerald Ford's Council of Economic Advisers, led by Alan Greenspan, acknowledged that productivity growth had slowed somewhat, but still estimated that the sustainable growth rate of the economy was a decent 3.5 percent per year.

However, the rise in physical and human capital didn't translate into higher productivity. From 1976 to 1982, for example, nonfarm business productivity rose at a minuscule 0.5 percent per year.

Economists have devoted endless papers to trying to explain the productivity slowdown, citing everything from increased regulation to a big influx of younger, less-skilled workers into the labor force.

But one simple explanation that economists dismissed too easily is technological failure. In particular, the two leading technological innovations of the 1960s—nuclear power and space travel—unexpectedly turned out to be major disappointments. We'll go into this in more detail in the next chapter. Suffice it here to say that the energy crisis of the 1970s would have taken a very different turn if nuclear power had delivered on its promise of power "too cheap to meter," as had been predicted in its early years. There might still have been lines for gasoline, but the nation would not have had a major energy scare. President Jimmy Carter's admonition to turn down home thermostats to 65 would have been unnecessary if cheap electric heating had been available.

Equally distressing was the failure of space travel to pay off big. Space was the nation's major R&D objective for the period between 1962 and 1972, with space-related activities absorbing almost 60 percent of nondefense government R&D spending in that period. In technical terms, the program was a success, since the U.S. was able to put astronauts on the moon. In economic terms, however, it was a total failure, with very little to show for all of that R&D spending in terms of spin-offs.

The economic failure of space travel and nuclear power could not have been anticipated. However, taken together, they had major macroeconomic effects.

Similarly, it was the unexpected success of the Internet that confounded economic forecasters in the 1990s. In the second half of the 1990s, for example, economists at the International Monetary Fund consistently expected that Europe would grow faster than the U.S. because of factors such as investment in physical capital. Unfortunately for the accuracy of their forecasts, the U.S.

got a big boost from technology that Europe didn't get. In fact, the U.S. grew faster than Europe every year from 1992 to 2000. In the end, technological change turned out to be a more important force than capital accumulation.

TABLE 3: ECONOMIC SINS AGAINST GROWTH

1. IGNORING TECHNOLOGY

Omitting technological change distorts discussions of long-term economic policy, since technology drives much of long-term productivity growth.

EXAMPLES:

MARTIN FELDSTEIN	President of the National Bureau of Economic Research and former chairman of the Council of Economic Advisers
MILTON FRIEDMAN	Winner of the Nobel Prize in Economics

2. BELITTLING TECHNOLOGY

Dismissing the importance of technology, or minimizing its ability to influence growth, makes it harder to get support for R&D spending.

EXAMPLES:

ALAN BLINDER	Former vice chairman of the Federal Reserve
PAUL KRUGMAN	*New York Times* columnist
N. GREGORY MANKIW	Current chairman of the Council of Economic Advisers

3. MISGUIDED POLICIES

Focusing on savings and investment as the major engines of economic growth encourages politicians to adopt policies that will add at most a couple of tenths of a percentage point to long-term growth rates.

EXAMPLES:

MARTIN FELDSTEIN	President of the National Bureau of Economic Research and former chairman of the Council of Economic Advisers
PAUL KRUGMAN	*New York Times* columnist
N. GREGORY MANKIW	Current chairman of the Council of Economic Advisers

Deficit Hawks, Liberals, Moralists, and Environmentalists: More Enemies of Exuberant Growth

> We remain, in part, appalled by the consequences of
> our ingenuity.
>> Elting Morison
>> *Men, Machines, and Modern Times* (1966)

It is unfair and inaccurate to single out economists as the sole skeptics of exuberant growth. Liberals complain that technology-driven growth is increasing inequality in the U.S., and doing nothing to help growth overseas. Environmentalists worry about the effects of fast growth on global warming, the impact of new technologies such as genetically modified foods, and the danger that global economic growth is putting too much stress on the environment.

The opposition toward exuberant growth comes from the right as well. Deficit hawks worry that people are blind to the long-term entitlement problem, and that the U.S. is sacrificing the future for the present. And there has been massive hostility to the cultural effects of the Internet. Between 1996 and 2000, Congress passed three anti-Internet pornography laws—the Communications Decency Act of 1996, the Child Online Protection Act of 1998, and the Children's Internet Protection Act, enacted in late 2000.

The breadth of the opposition reflects the provocative nature of exuberant growth. Far more than cautious growth, exuberant growth challenges the status quo and evokes deeply held feelings about what's right and what's normal.

THE IMMORALITY OF BORROWING

Deficit hawks, like most economists, are opposed to budget deficits. But for the true deficit hawks, it's a moral issue, not just an economic one. They are opposed to government borrowing, period—with little consideration about whether the money is being spent on something useful, such as education, R&D, or infrastructure. In this sense, deficit hawks are enemies of growth because they have a different set of goals.

Such fiscal conservatives are a minority, but a vocal one. For them, prudence is a cardinal virtue, and building up debt is a character flaw, no matter how productively the money is used.

The argument against budget deficits is based on moral concerns as much as economic ones. One of the leading deficit hawks, Peter Peterson—a former secretary of commerce and author of multiple books warning of the coming fiscal crisis—testified before Congress in April 2003, saying:

> When such deficits are incurred in order to fund a rising
> transfer from young to old, they also constitute an injustice
> against future generations.

This is the language of morality, rather than economics. From this perspective, taking on debt is wrong because it reflects profligacy and wastefulness, and shows that the government is out of control.

In his 2003 book, *In an Uncertain World*, Robert Rubin, treasury secretary under Bill Clinton and also a well-known advocate against budget deficits, made a similar point about how reducing the budget deficit was more about psychology than economics:

> There was nothing scientific about how much deficit reduction would have credibility and create a real economic impact. In a $6.6 trillion economy, a few billion more or less–a small fraction of 1 percent of GDP–shouldn't make a big difference. . . .
>
> In retrospect, the effect of the Clinton economic plan on business and consumer confidence may have been even more important than the effect on interest rates.

Deficit hawks also find the thought of waste abhorrent. From their perspective, the $600 toilet seat–spending more money than you have to–is the mark of a spendthrift culture. One of the great deficit hawks of all time, Senator William Proxmire, started giving out his Golden Fleece Award in 1975 to agencies that wasted taxpayer money. Out of about 150 Fleeces, Proxmire gave scientists about two dozen, including one to NASA in 1978 for wanting to look for signs of extraterrestrial life.

Unfortunately, this antiwaste, antidebt mind-set is inimical to innovation, which inevitably requires going down a lot of dead-end roads before finding success. Almost by definition, a lot of money is wasted trying a lot of different possibilities that don't work out, or starting a lot of businesses that fail. From the perspective of a deficit hawk, exuberant growth is intensely disturbing.

The heyday of the deficit hawks was the 1980s, when the U.S. economy seemed unable to keep pace with Japan and Germany. Both of those countries saved and invested a much higher share of GDP than the U.S. did.

It seemed very simple. If the U.S. wanted to grow, what it had to do was cut the budget deficit and increase national savings and investment. If we didn't do that—well, then we were nearsighted gluttons who deserved what we got.

Thus, Benjamin Friedman, a Harvard economist, argued in 1988 that government borrowing

> violated the basic moral principle that had bound each
> generation of Americans to the next since the founding of
> the republic: that men and women should work and eat,
> earn and spend, both privately and collectively, so that
> their children and their children's children would inherit
> a better world.

However, much to the surprise of the deficit hawks, the U.S. was not punished in the 1990s for its spendthrift behavior. Instead, it was the big savers—Japan and Germany—that suffered, while the U.S. did spectacularly well. Meanwhile, the U.S. was able to grow its way out of the budget deficits of the early 1990s.

In fact, there is little convincing evidence that moderate deficits have a harmful economic impact, either today or in the future. Consider the experience of the last few years. In August 2001, the economy was in recession, the global economy was struggling, capital spending was very weak, and the Congressional Budget Office (CBO) was projecting a cumulative $3.4 trillion budget surplus for the next 10 years. By January 2004, the economy was gaining speed, and the CBO was projecting a $1.9 trillion deficit for the next 10 years. That's a swing of $5.3 trillion.

But interest rates did not go up, as deficit hawks would have predicted. In August 2001, the interest rate on the 10-year bond was just under 5 percent–higher than it was in January 2004.

How can all this borrowing not have any effect on interest rates in the U.S.? The answer is very simple. Capital markets are global these days. We can tap into savings not just in the U.S., but all around the world. In that context, the U.S. budget deficit consumes about 9 percent of global savings–not chicken feed, but not a big deal either.

Instead, belief in the negative impact of deficits is simply a matter of faith. Consider what Mankiw–a true believer in savings–has written about the impact of deficits on interest rates. After reviewing the empirical work on the topic, he and his coauthor are forced to admit that "this literature has typically supported the . . . view that budget deficits have no effect on interest rates."

But, undeterred, Mankiw simply states that "the results are simply too hard to swallow," adding that "In this case, the debate over theory is more persuasive than the debate over evidence." So much for economics being an empirical science.

It's important to remember that the deficit hawk argument against exuberant growth is less a matter of economics than it is a matter of morals. Prudence and savings is the moral course to take, even if it produces slower growth.

THE LIBERAL HERESY

Deficit hawks have historically been mostly conservative (Bob Rubin aside), but liberals have a love-hate relationship with exuberant growth as well. On the one hand, there is no doubt that faster growth pushes up wages at the bottom, lowers poverty rates, and provides more resources for social programs. That was true for the 1990s boom, and most of the gains were preserved even after the recession. That's an important achievement.

But there's a strong liberal antipathy to exuberant growth, which can be summarized by a simple syllogism. Technological change increases income inequality, increases insecurity, and erodes the power of skilled labor, by automating or "deskilling" jobs. Income inequality and insecurity are bad, and so is reducing worker power. Therefore, technological change is bad.

There's little doubt that inequality has increased in recent years. For example, the share of total income going to the top 5 percent of American households rose from 21 percent in 1993 to 22.4 percent in 2001. That's a small but significant increase.

Similarly, even during the boom of the 1990s, it seems clear that there was an enormous amount of turmoil in the job market, as the economy remolded itself to the new realities. Figures from the Bureau of Labor Statistics show that the number of gross job losses—declines in employment at existing establishments—actually was higher in 1999 and 2000 than earlier in the decade, despite the boom. According to research by Princeton economist Henry Farber, people who lost their job typically absorbed a big drop in earnings, even if they quickly found a new job. For example, in the period 1997–99, college-educated job losers suffered an overall loss of earnings of 20 percent. "It is clear that job losers fall substantially beyond non-losers in earnings," writes Farber.

The hostility of many liberals to exuberant growth has been augmented by a distrust of globalization, which seems to go hand in hand with technological change. The fear is that globalization is making workers in developing nations worse off, not better off, by exposing them to rapacious multinationals. At the same time, the threat of cheap labor is being used to beat down wages in the U.S.

And finally, there's the intangible impact of all the corporate and Wall Street corruption. Even among liberals who appreciate technology, there is a pervasive sense that the technology-driven New Economy was a bit of a sham, or worse, a scam perpetuated by the rich to take advantage of the poor and gullible. Consider, for example, Joseph Stiglitz, the Nobel Prize–winning economist who served as chief economist at the World Bank and head of the Council of Economic Advisers in the Clinton Administration. In his 2003 book, *The Roaring Nineties*, Stiglitz argues that the U.S. underinvests in research, which he believes has a high rate of return. That alone would take him out of the category of "enemies of growth." Nevertheless he also writes skeptically about the 1990s, saying that:

> toward the end of the decade, what seemed to be the dawn
> of a new era began to look more and more like one of those
> short bursts of economic activity, or hyperactivity,
> inevitably followed by a bust, which had marked capitalism
> for two hundred years.

Others went much further in their skepticism. Journalist Jeffrey Madrick, in his 2002 book, *Why Economies Grow*, wrote about the late 1990s:

> The belief in technological determinism–that technology
> was the principal determinant of growth–reached its height
> in those years. . . . It was . . . used by Wall Street to promote
> extraordinary levels of speculation in securities; and
> eventually accepted and advocated in its simple form even
> by some economists. . . . The new economy was essentially
> an invention of the media and Wall Street.

A similar sentiment was expressed by Thomas Frank in his 2000 bestseller, *One Market under God.* Frank wrote:

> The new era came with a real world price tag. . . . The price was the destruction of the social contract of mid-century, the middle class republic itself . . . we countenanced the reduction of millions to lives of casual employment without healthcare or the most elementary sort of workplace rights.

Then Frank went on to sum up his skepticism in this way:

> The great euphoria of the late nineties was never as much about the return of good times as it was the giddy triumph of one America over another, of their "New Economy" over our New Deal.

The schizophrenic attitude of liberalism toward growth has been present since at least the days of Franklin Roosevelt and the quintessential liberal program, the New Deal. During the campaign of 1932, the incumbent Republican president, Herbert Hoover, presented himself as the champion of technology-based growth. As historian Robert Collins writes in his 2000 book, *More,* Hoover would explain to his campaign audiences that

> we are yet but on the frontiers of development of science . . . and . . . invention.

By contrast, during his campaign, Roosevelt painted a picture of a mature economy without much room for rapid growth. "Our industrial plant is built," Roosevelt said in a September 1932 speech. "Our last frontier has long since been reached, and there is practically no more free land." This was the traditional liberal position–pessimistic about capitalism.

Roosevelt and his advisors took office operating under the assumption that the economy was stuck in slow growth on a permanent basis. Wrote Collins:

> The emphasis of so many New Deal programs on "security"–indeed, perhaps the most important thread unifying what critics characterized as the New Deal hodgepodge–bespoke a similarly pessimistic reading of the nation's present condition and future chances. Many liberals came to view massive unemployment as a permanent problem.

But after being in office a year or so, Roosevelt began shifting toward a new strain of pro-growth liberalism. Economic growth, rather than an expression of rampant capitalism, became a way of funding social programs and helping the poor and unemployed. This was the political genius of the New Deal and Keynesian economics: Combining government economic stimulus with a real safety net for the poor–which had never existed before–tamed capitalism, and made growth safe for liberals.

After World War II, pro-growth liberalism continued to be a strong political movement in the 1950s and through the first half of the 1960s. In many ways, the intellectual foundations of pro-growth liberalism came from Simon Kuznets, a Harvard economist who was later to win the Nobel Prize in Economics in 1971 for his work in development and economic growth. Looking at the history of different countries, Kuznets observed that inequality rose as a country first started on the path to economic development, and then fell as it moved into more advanced industrialization. In other words, Kuznets' Law, as it was called, suggested that the past abuses of capitalism could actually be corrected by more growth.

The experiences of the 1960s seemed to support the idea that faster growth was good for the poor. During the decade—which had one of the fastest growth rates on record—incomes and wages soared, the poverty rate fell from 18 percent to under 10 percent, and the share of income going to the poor rose.

Nevertheless, there were plenty of liberals who were starting to become uncomfortable with growth. That was the meaning of John Kenneth Galbraith's *The Affluent Society*, originally published in 1958, which argued that the U.S. economy was rich enough, and needed to devote itself to noneconomic goals. In 1959, Arthur Schlesinger Jr. wrote that "today we dwell in an economy of abundance," and argued for the need to move to "qualitative liberalism."

The implication was that we needed to care more about the quality of life, and about taking care of the poor, than aiming for higher growth.

The liberal opponents of growth gained strength in the 1960s, nourished in part by the political turmoil of the decade. Economic growth looked a lot less desirable when one of its main fuels seemed to be military spending on the Vietnam War.

But it wasn't until the 1970s and 1980s that the liberal faith in growth was fully eroded. The problem was that Kuznets' Law began to operate in reverse. For roughly 20 years—from the mid-1970s to the mid-1990s—the economy grew, but the poor suffered. Wages for most people, adjusted for inflation, fell. The poverty rate skyrocketed, and inequality increased. Most significant, the wage gap between college-educated and high school–educated workers widened dramatically.

It became an article of faith among many liberals that this widening wage gap was caused by technology and globalization, the very factors that brought growth. The unions—one of the traditional bases of the liberal movement—were very suspicious of technological change, because automation seemed to be primarily used by companies to reduce the power of workers. Globalization, too, seemed primarily to mean moving factories to countries with cheaper labor and less restrictive work rules.

This skeptical attitude toward technology and globalization showed up in the textbooks written by liberal economists. For example, in their textbook *The Economic Problem,* Robert Heilbroner and James Galbraith (son of John Kenneth Galbraith) characterized technology as "a genie that capitalism let out of the bottle; it has ever since refused to go back in." Later in the textbook they laid out the negative consequences of technology:

> By common consent, the new technology brings unprecedented threats. It is hugely destructive (nuclear explosives), risky (genetic engineering), of dubious profitability (space) and possibly disruptive—the arrival of the automated office and the robotized assembly line, for example, may swell the ranks of the unemployed with displaced white-collar as well as blue-collar workers.

In his 1996 book about urban unemployment, *When Work Disappears,* William Julius Wilson points to technology as a key reason for increasing income inequality.

> It is important to recognize that much of the sharp rise in inner-city joblessness in the United States and the growth of unemployment in Europe and Canada stems from the swift technological changes in the global economy.

True, there were periodic attempts to create a new generation of pro-growth liberals. One of the first came in the early 1980s, when the so-called Atari Democrats–led by Congressmen Tim Wirth and Gary Hart–advocated supporting high-tech industries as a way of spurring growth. Unfortunately, the Atari Democrats never really took off as a political movement, undercut by the fact that tech jobs seemed to be flowing overseas as fast as nontech jobs in the 1980s, and that Japan was challenging the U.S. lead in semi-conductors. The added complication that corporate namesake Atari cut 2,500 jobs in 1983 and shifted production abroad didn't help the cause either.

Liberals remained quite skeptical of technology-driven growth, even when the New Economy started picking up in the middle of the 1990s. Liberal think tanks such as the Economic Policy Institute regularly disputed even the possibility of an acceleration of growth. And President Clinton's Council of Economic Advisers, too, was very reluctant to jump aboard the New Economy bandwagon, consistently issuing low-growth forecasts through most of the 1990s. As late as January 1999, the council was predicting 2 percent growth for the year ahead, reflecting a generally pessimistic attitude toward the economy's capabilities.

SPIRITUAL POVERTY

Liberals object to exuberant growth because it ostensibly hurts the poor or less-educated, but there are a different set of noneconomic objections as well. There's a widespread concern–often voiced at sermons at churches and synagogues, but held more widely–that an accumulation of material goods, even new and different ones, does not lead to a satisfying life. The fear is that rising income does not compensate for a lack of contact with friends or a feeling of rootlessness. And a belief that consumerism–the giant malls, the arrays of expensive items–adds nothing to human happiness.

As Neil Postman, the late critic of technology, wrote, technology "makes life easier, cleaner, and longer," but "it creates a culture without a moral foundation" and undermines the very things that make life worth living.

Despite the fact that the second half of the 1990s was clearly economically superior to the second half of the 1980s—lower unemployment, higher wages—surveys show that happiness was lower in the 1990s. In 1998, for example, 33 percent of the people interviewed by the General Social Survey, one of the largest regular surveys of attitudes, were "very happy." In 1988, that percentage was 36 percent. Similarly, the number of "not too happy" people was lower in 1988.

Particular aspects of technological change seem to challenge widely held values. The ease of downloading pornographic images from the Internet seems to threaten the ability of parents to control the exposure of their children to sexual images. Stem cell research—in part based on cells harvested from aborted fetuses—raises tough ethical questions, especially for people who are not comfortable with abortion.

Moral opposition to economic growth draws on a long history of such disquiet in Western civilization, reaching all the way back to the Greeks. In his book *The Mind and the Market*, historian Jerry Z. Muller notes that Aristotle saw commerce as morally debilitating.

> Unlike more moral pursuits—the pursuit of wealth lacks any natural, intrinsic limit and is hence prone to excess. Those engaged in commerce for money thus have a propensity to *pleonexia* (greediness or overreaching); they tend to devote their lives to gaining more and more without limit or reflective purpose.

The early Christian Church had an equally jaundiced view of commerce and wealth. Saint Thomas Aquinas believed, for example, that acquisitiveness was a mark of covetness or pride. For him,

> wealth was an act of fortuitous circumstance, which the recipient was to accept calmly and dispose of as quickly as possible in good works and charity. Too frequent or too intimate contact with material prosperity was living dangerously, and a good Christian saw to it that he did not needlessly imperil his soul.

Today, warnings to focus on the spiritual life, rather than material things, are still a staple of sermons in churches and synagogues across the country. One indication: In 2001, the Council of Bishops of the United Methodist Church, a denomination with roughly 8 million members, published a missive that denounced the "the spiritual poverty of the prosperous."

But the disgust with materialism is not restricted to the religious. The idea that our economy is based on the consumption of empty calories—buying things we don't need, hyped up by advertising—strikes a chord in all of us. Every time our kids whine for the latest expensive toy or demand an expensive fashionable piece of clothing, we have the feeling that solid values have been replaced by demand driven by television or by the Internet.

This instinctive revulsion is backed up by a mountain of research that shows that, once national income reaches about $10,000 per person, further increases seem to have a minimal impact on national happiness. As Daniel Sarewitz, a scholar at Columbia University's Center for Science, Policy, and Outcomes, wrote in his 1996 book, *Frontiers of Illusion:*

The past fifty years have shown that the linkage between scientific progress and societal well-being is highly attenuated. . . . Knowledge and innovation grow at breathtaking rates, and so does the scale of the problems that face humanity.

In his 2003 book, *Enough,* Bill McKibben, author of the 1989 bestseller *The End of Nature,* writes:

Is it possible that our technological reach is very nearly sufficient? That our lives, at least in the West, are sufficiently comfortable?

McKibben argues that past technological advances had unfortunate side effects:

The invention of the car offered the freedom of mobility, at the cost of giving up the small, coherent physical universes most people had inhabited. The invention of radio and television allowed the unlimited choices of a national or global culture, but undermined the local life that had long persisted . . . the pill and the sexual revolution freed us from the formerly inherent burdens of sex, but also often reduced it to the merely "casual." . . . We've tried hard to fill the hole left when community disappeared, with "traditional values" and evangelical churches, with back-to-the-land communities and New Age rituals. But those frantic stirrings serve mostly to highlight our radical loneliness.

To one degree or another, we all worry about the negative effects of technology in our daily lives. We complain about drivers who talk on their cell phones and don't watch where they are going; we complain about spam taking too much time when we log on; we worry about the effect of violent video games on our children—these are all moral arguments against growth, not economic arguments.

ENVIRONMENTALISM AND THE FEAR OF THE FUTURE

In theory, technological change could just as easily help the environment as hurt it. It's quite easy to imagine genetically engineered bugs that eat up oil spills. Countries in the early stages of industrialization are often more polluted than more advanced countries, with coal-burning steel plants, for example, putting out enormous amounts of air pollution. And one could, in principle, even imagine a nuclear power plant that was much safer than current models, while putting out very few of the gases that contribute to global warming.

But as a general rule, environmentalists have concerns about technological change and exuberant growth. Their objections can be separated into two groups. First, they worry about the consequences of new technologies, both on the natural world and on humans. That includes the possibility of disastrous global warming. Second, some environmentalists simply do not accept the idea that economic growth is the right goal to strive for.

The first group of objectors—which includes organizations such as Worldwatch, the Sierra Club, and Greenpeace—have consistently raised legitimate concerns about the health and safety consequences of new technologies, running from nuclear power to gene-modified food to nanotechnology. These objections represent an important hurdle that any new technology has to cross, as we will see in Chapter 6. In fact, such critics of technology are an essential part of the process of shaping the next step along the economic road.

Even the debate over global warming is not necessarily inimical to exuberant growth. The concern over reducing the emission of greenhouse gases is accelerating the development of alternative technologies such as hybrid cars. Similarly, if concern about global warming accelerates the development of affordable solar power, that could dramatically transform the energy sector and unleash the next wave of technologically driven growth. As the *State of the World 2002* from the Worldwatch Institute observes:

> The potential of new technologies and policies to slow
> climate change has grown dramatically.... Advances are
> taking place in a wide range of technologies that are in
> varying stages of development.

Well-known environmental advocates such as Jeremy Rifkin and Amory Lovins argue for the shift to a hydrogen economy, in which hydrogen would replace fossil fuels wherever possible, including as the motive force for automobiles. Because hydrogen produces only water when used to provide energy, it's far less polluting than fossil fuels. Moreover, at least in principle, it's more efficient. Lovins writes:

> A hydrogen fuel-cell car can therefore convert hydrogen
> energy into motion about 2–3 times as efficiently as a
> normal car converts gasoline energy into motion.

For Lovins, Rifkin, and others, technology is the solution, as long as it is the right technology. Such environmentalists are more comfortable with technological change than most economists are.

But the other strand of environmental thought is far more antitechnology and antigrowth. The objections are often phrased in terms of what is known as the precautionary principle: "When an activity raises threats of harm to the environment or human health, precautionary measures should be taken even if some cause and effect relationships are not fully established scientifically." This principle is often interpreted as simply calling for more safety tests on new chemicals. However, it can also go as far as a hostility to most new technologies. As one advocate put it:

> The precautionary principle requires us to assign the
> burden of proof to those who want to introduce a new
> technology, particularly in cases where there is little or
> no established need or benefit and where the hazards are
> serious and irreversible. It is up to perpetrators to prove
> that the technology is safe "beyond reasonable doubt."

The use of the term "perpetrators" for people trying to introduce new technologies is certainly a sign of the underlying attitude toward change. Whether you believe that it's a good idea or not, it's clear that the end result of the precautionary principle, fully applied, would be to sharply slow down innovation and growth. "If someone had evaluated the risk of fire right after it was invented," Julian Morris of the Institute of Economic Affairs in London told *Scientific American* in January 2001, "they may well have decided to eat their food raw."

A big part of the dilemma is that many of the problems stemming from a new technology—and how to solve them—are not seen until the technology is in use. As we will see in the next chapter, innovation, by its nature, is highly unpredictable. So it would be almost impossible to give a guarantee ahead of time that a new technology was safe.

Most of the applications of a new technology are also unknown at the time of its invention. That means the precautionary principle—facing unknown benefits and unknown costs—will almost always tend to lean against introducing new technologies.

The precautionary principle can be applied to advances in health care as well. In a 2003 book, Daniel Callahan, one of the founders of the Hastings Center and its president until 1996, worries about the potentially negative effects on society of extending life spans, and argues that such advances should be scrutinized in advance: "To drop a new and far-reaching technology on our society, or any society, simply because people would buy it would be irresponsible." Callahan goes on to argue:

> There is no reason whatever for government-supported research aimed at maximizing or optimizing life spans . . . nor is there any reason to encourage the private sector to pursue it either . . . there would be every reason to put moral, political, and social pressure on the private sector not to move on in the research unless it took part in a major national effort to work through in *advance* the likely problems that success might bring everyone.

The logical extension of the precautionary principle is the steady- or stationary-state economy—that is, an economy with little or no growth in output per person. Since the 1970s, one of the leading prophets of the steady-state economy has been Herman Daly, a professor at the University of Maryland, and a former senior economist at the World Bank.

In his book *Steady State Economics,* Daly argued that "a steady state economy is a necessary and desirous future state of affairs." He added that "a U.S. style high-mass consumption, growth dominated economy" for the entire world "is impossible." Daly quoted approvingly from Aleksandr Solzhenitsyn, who said, "Economic growth is not only unnecessary but ruinous."

But steady state economics is more than just a matter of slow growth. In Daly's view, scientific progress verges on the immoral, by displacing God. Daly wrote:

> The steady state view conceives of man as a fallible creature whose hope lies in the benevolence of his Creator not in the excellence of his own creations. Scientific growth mania sees man as a potentially infallible creator whose hope lies in his marvelous scientific creativity and not in any superstitions about an unobservable creator.

In this view, exuberant growth is actually heresy. Such extreme views are not shared by most environmentalists. Nevertheless, replace the term "God" or "Creator" with Nature, and it gets closer to the commonly held beliefs of environmentalism.

CONCLUSION

We have come full circle, from the technologically challenged economist to the technophobic environmentalists. These represent a formidable set of opponents for exuberant growth and technological change.

More broadly, it's impossible to understand the debates over economic policy without realizing that fast growth is simply not the primary goal for many participants. That's why exuberant growth is more fragile than we think.

CHAPTER 6

The Next Big Breakthrough? Biotech, Telecom, Energy, Nanotechnology, and Space

Exuberant growth is transformative, in the sense that it opens up new possibilities, both social and economic. And exuberant growth is, well, exuberant—it creates a sense of excitement that is hard to duplicate any other way.

At the same time, the enemies of exuberant growth are many and varied. Their arguments resonate precisely because they contain powerful elements of truth. Exuberant growth does in fact have major negative economic, social, and environmental consequences. Technology can increase income inequality and disrupt jobs; it can undercut community and decrease social cohesion; it can damage the environment and create unimaginable medical hazards.

Those of us who support exuberant growth face three interlinked problems. First, we need to find new technologies that are potent enough to propel growth forward, and to have a major impact on the way we live our lives. That's not an easy task. Second, any potential breakthrough technologies must be developed and brought to market, in the face of high costs of research and development, the inevitable failures and blind alleys, and the often-justifiable resistance from the enemies of growth. Third, the negative consequences of technological change must be ameliorated. The average person should be able to support exuberant growth without fearing that he or she will be destroyed by the side effects. Without such a social compact, the popular support for exuberant growth will erode.

Despite these problems, another technology-driven boom is not just possible but likely. This chapter will show that there are plenty of new technologies bubbling beneath the surface that have the potential to drive exuberant growth. The development of these technologies has been fueled by a dramatic rise in global civilian R&D spending over the last decade. Moreover, the number of trained scientists and engineers around the world has taken a big jump, especially with increased spending on higher education in India and China. More resources devoted to technological exploration means a greater chance of finding something that works.

Still, innovation is profoundly uncertain, no matter how many scientists and how much money are thrown at a problem. It is impossible to predict which one of the technologies under development will succeed. The process of uncovering and developing new technologies is both very risky and very expensive, and requires a willingness to pursue multiple lines of research simultaneously.

The next chapter shows how the U.S. has developed a financial system for encouraging and financing potential new breakthroughs—even expensive ones. As a result, unlike any other country, the U.S. can put substantial resources into pursuing multiple potential breakthroughs simultaneously—funding research, start-ups, and new product development, as well as absorbing the financial pain of failures. It's like putting down bets on more than one number at the roulette wheel–the odds of winning go way up. In this case, it means there's a good chance that one of the new technologies will turn out to be compelling enough to hurdle the economic, technological, and regulatory barriers.

THE NEXT BIG THING?

The first obstacle to continued exuberant growth can be summed up in the question: What Is the Next Big Thing? Skeptics argue that the technological revolution ignited by the Internet was a once-in-a-lifetime event, and that to hope for another innovation of a similar magnitude anytime soon would be misguided and tragically foolhardy.

After the experience of being burned by overhyped technologies in the 1990s, many investors–and journalists as well–are rightfully wary of any claims of a new technological revolution. It wasn't just the tech and telecom busts that produced cynicism–biotech and alternative energy, too, went through several roller-coaster rides in which stock prices shot up because investors were certain that these technologies were finally about to explode. Then, when it became clear that the celebration was at best premature, the prices plummeted again. As the saying goes: "Fool me once, shame on you. Fool me twice, shame on me."

The pessimism is all the more understandable as we look across much of the economy. In the Age of the Internet, there are many more industries that seem stuck in a time warp. The internal combustion engine has powered cars for more than 100 years, ever since Gottlieb Daimler and Karl Benz, working separately, invented successful gasoline-powered vehicles in Germany in the

1880s. Virtually all the new electrical-power-generating capacity in the next decade is expected to come from gas-powered turbines, which were first put into use for that purpose in 1959. And many factories today look very similar to pictures from 30 or 40 years ago, with the exception of less clutter and inventory lying around.

In fact, while computers and the Internet have transformed the communications and information industries, the impact of information technology on other parts of the economy has been incremental rather than revolutionary. For example, computers reduce the cost of paperwork and back-office processing for hospitals, but have no direct effect on finding a better treatment for lung cancer, say. The Internet does nothing for the fundamental questions of finding new sources of energy that are cheap and also environmentally sound.

What's needed is a breakthrough that is capable of revolutionizing one of the major sectors of the economy. That tough criterion helps us identify possible candidates for the Next Big Thing (see Table 4). The most logical technology to transform health care—which accounts for roughly 10 percent of private sector labor compensation—is biotech. Any one of several energy innovations—including fuel cells or solar power—could dramatically invigorate energy generation or distribution, where technology has been basically stalled for decades. Manufacturing could be revolutionized if nanotechnology—which is basically a set of techniques for building up products from the atomic level—ever bears fruit. And space travel—which so far is technologically feasible but economically unviable—entices with its promise of a new frontier.

Any of these potential innovations, if they bear fruit over the next few years, is capable of triggering another round of exuberant growth. Like the 1990s, it would be a period of enormous excitement, complete with another stock market boom and a vibrant labor market. The question, though, is which one.

TABLE 4: THE NEXT BREAKTHROUGH?

SECTOR	LAST MAJOR SUCCESSFUL TECHNOLOGICAL ADVANCE	POSSIBLE CANDIDATE
Communications	Internet	Advanced telecom
Manufacturing/materials	Plastics	Nanotechnology
Health	Many	Biotechnology
Energy	Electricity, gas turbines	Fuel cells, solar power, nuclear power
Transportation	Airplanes	Space

PROFOUND UNCERTAINTY

An exuberant innovation-driven economy requires a different mind-set about growth than a cautious economy. A cautious economy is like a well-paved highway. The accumulation of physical and human capital is predictable, as is the process of incremental improvements to existing products, and you have a good idea of your final destination. By contrast, exuberant growth is like taking a vehicle off-road into new territory. The path is bumpy, and you can never quite tell where you are going to end up.

Innovation is profoundly unpredictable. Any new technology has to pass substantial and very real hurdles: The new technology has to work reliably, it has to make economic sense, it has to be safe, and consumers have to accept it. Nuclear power, for example, is the classic case of a technology that worked in the engineering sense, but in practice was not economic or acceptable to consumers.

In an exuberant economy, we have to acclimate ourselves to the fact that we cannot tell which innovation is going to pay off first. First, original ideas for new products and innovations do not arrive on a regular schedule. An innovation may not be feasible in practice until other advances have been made, or it may not be clear how it can best be used. And even an idea that is feasible may require a lot of fine-tuning to work. "Pervasive uncertainty characterizes not only basic research, where it is generally acknowledged," wrote Nathan Rosenberg, a Stanford University economist who has studied the development of technology, "but the realm of product design and new product development as well."

As a result, our ability to predict the Next Big Thing is almost nonexistent. History shows that it is hard to see a major innovation coming even just before it hits. The Next Big Thing does not come with flashing lights attached to it and a big sign saying "This is it!" Sometimes, like the Internet, it sidles up on us in small little steps. Other times, like the laser, it takes years after the technological leap has happened before its value is recognized.

In fact, we can even go a step further and say that there are low odds of any particular innovation or technology working out. That applies, incidentally, to the technologies that are integral parts of our life today, such as electricity. We accept the web of power lines running through our houses and in the streets as necessary and safe. But in the 1880s and 1890s, when electricity was first introduced, there was widespread fear of the new technology. Politicians, scientists, and business leaders worried about the possibility of electrocution, of steam boilers blowing up at the central power plants, of fires. When Thomas Edison was building the first power plant in lower Manhattan in 1883, he was attacked by the national press and by experts who believed that gas lighting would ultimately win out.

Of course, now the safety of electricity seems assured, and the notion of gas lighting seems far more dangerous. Similarly, the advantages of automobiles have more than overwhelmed their downsides, which include over 40,000 fatalities per year from auto accidents, and the need to store large quantities of gasoline–a very flammable and potentially explosive substance–in residential areas (not to mention in fast-moving vehicles).

Stories of the early days of the microprocessor make it clear that it was quite difficult to get high levels of reliability from such tiny circuits so close together. Most of all, when Gordon Moore first predicted in 1965 that the number of transistors on a silicon chip would double every 18 months or two years, no one, least of all Moore, would have expected the prediction to hold for the next four decades. His original forecast was for only 10 years.

It's hard to tell, however, the exact ratio of failures to successes. Scientists do not generally publish their failed experiments; corporations generally do not publicize the products that never made it out of their R&D labs. One measure of innovative uncertainty comes from the experiences of venture capitalists. Most venture capital (VC) firms fund a portfolio of start-up firms. Out of those, the rule of thumb is that the VC firm is doing well if three out of 10 survive, and one out of every 10 investments turns into a big winner. This is a long-term average, of course. During the boom of the late 1990s, it seemed like every venture investment turned to gold, so that their hit rate was a lot higher than one out of 10. But factor in the disaster of the bust, and it seems like the original rule of thumb is still pretty close to the truth.

Another way of getting at the uncertainty of innovation is to look at the track record of technology forecasts. In 1967, Herman Kahn and Anthony Wiener of the Hudson Institute made a set of technology predictions for the year 2000. It turns out that they were right in about roughly one-third of their predictions. In general, the information technology predictions, such as direct broadcasts from satellites to home receivers, have come true; the energy and transportation predictions, such as "individual flying platforms," have tended to fall short; and the record on the biology and health predictions is mixed (some predictions, such as "new and relatively effective counterinsurgency techniques," are hard to assess).

It's equally interesting to look at another set of technology forecasts that Kahn published in 1982, in a book entitled *The Coming Boom*. Kahn predicted technology breakthroughs in 10 areas, including energy, space, and biotechnology. Once again, the hit rate was about one-third, with reality surpassing his predictions in the two info-tech-related areas: semiconductors and automation of home, office, and factories. However, it turned out that it wasn't necessary for all his predictions to be right–even having just those two big winners was enough to drive economic growth.

BUBBLING BENEATH THE SURFACE

The fact is, the breakthrough product or company may already be out there. Even in today's modern economy–with its so-called overload of information–it's possible to miss the importance of critical innovations. While the business press was blamed for overhyping new technologies in the 1990s, it's equally true that journalists have a terrible track record in spotting the real breakthroughs.

The most compelling case of the experts and the media simply missing good news is Cisco Systems, one of the great companies of our time. Cisco was founded in 1984 and in 1986 started shipping its first commercial routers, which connected networks to other networks. In other words, Cisco made the plumbing for the Internet. The company went public in February 1990, and its stock tripled in price in the first year. For a while during the boom, it was the largest company in the U.S., in terms of market capitalization.

What did investors know about Cisco before it went public? Almost nothing—it wasn't even a blip on the radar screen. Up until the months before the company went public, there was hardly any significant mention of Cisco in any of the major print publications. That includes *BusinessWeek, Fortune, Forbes,* the *New York Times,* and even the *San Francisco Chronicle,* which is known for its intensive coverage of Silicon Valley, where Cisco was based.

Let's reiterate that. One of the most successful companies of our time received next to no coverage in the major press up to the moment it went public. At the same time, there was plenty of media attention lavished on companies that either no longer exist or were total failures. For example, in the last two months of 1989, *BusinessWeek* wrote about the revival of AT&T (which never happened), and such computer makers as Data General, Wang Laboratories, and Convex Computer, which all struggled in the 1990s before being acquired.

Cisco is not a special case. Journalists and experts also misjudged, badly, the potential success of eBay. The online auction company went public in September 1998. Over the previous year, it received almost no attention—and what little it did receive treated it as a glorified swap meet, fit only to trade Beanie Babies and the like. That description wasn't far off—at the time it went public, it had 35,000 Beanie Babies on offer. Some analysts worried that its business model was too easy to imitate. Of course, it turned out to be quite the opposite, as eBay's online auction was one of the few successful companies built during the dot-com era.

The implication is that the small company with the Next Big Thing could be out there right now, and we might not know about them. Or more precisely, it might be very difficult to distinguish them from all the other companies that will not succeed. In retrospect, of course, experts always claim that the nature of the technological leap was clear to them. But hindsight is 20-20.

PERVASIVE UNPREDICTABILITY

The best ideas all look obvious in retrospect, but at the time no one sees them. Take the 1928 discovery of penicillin by Alexander Fleming (who later won the Nobel Prize in Medicine). At the time of his discovery, scientists knew that some compounds had antimicrobial properties but no one had found an antibiotic that was both effective and safe. Even after Fleming published his result, it took another 10 years before the true value was recognized. Widespread use of penicillin did not start until the 1940s and required additional breakthroughs that warranted the Nobel Prize as well.

Or move closer into the present. The Internet as we know it today would not have been possible without the Web browser, which was originally proposed by Tim Berners-Lee of CERN research laboratory in Switzerland in 1989, and then turned into a working program by 1991. It's worth pointing out, however, that the software technology necessary to create the browser—so obvious in retrospect—had been available for years. Notes economic historian Joel Mokyr: "Macroinventions . . . do not seem to obey obvious laws, do not necessarily respond to incentives and defy most attempts to relate them to exogenous economic variables."

The difficulty of coming up with the original innovation is just the first level of unpredictability. The history of technology shows very clearly that even when a technological breakthrough occurs, it is often not recognized as such because no one can imagine its full set of applications. In 1877, telegraph giant Western Union turned down the chance to buy Alexander Graham Bell's telephone patent for $100,000 (roughly $1.7 million in today's dollars—not very much), greatly underestimating the future possibilities of the new technology. Within a year it became obvious to the executives at Western Union that they had made a tremendous mistake, and they launched a fruitless competition.

More than 100 years later, history came close to repeating

itself, as Microsoft nearly misjudged just how important the Internet would become. In 1994, most of Microsoft's executives–including the man at the top–were focused on launching the company's proprietary online service. The Internet was still a distinct second. "I wouldn't say it was clear it was going to explode over the next couple of years," chairman William H. Gates III told *BusinessWeek* in 1996. "If you'd asked me then if most TV ads will have URLs [Web addresses] in them, I would have laughed."

What's surprising is that even innovations that have broad and widespread uses today were originally thought of as being much narrower. As Nathan Rosenberg notes, the steam engine, patented in 1769 by James Watt, was for many years regarded mainly as a pump, useful for pumping water out of flooded mines. No one foresaw the more important applications of the steam engine in powering factories and railroads.

Part of the reason why forecasting is difficult is that even the best idea may not be feasible without complementary inventions, which are completely unpredictable as well. Leonardo da Vinci's notebooks are filled with drawings of things such as a kind of helicopter, which simply could not be built with the power sources or materials then available.

Sometimes it's even impossible to imagine beforehand what sort of additional innovations or developments would be necessary. One example: Building skyscrapers was not possible without the development of a workable and safe elevator. And while the basic idea of elevators had been around for literally centuries, the critical innovation didn't come until 1853 when Elisha Otis came up with a workable idea for putting a safety brake on elevators, to prevent falling if the cable should break–something that in retrospect seems simple.

Another example is the laser. The first working laser was demonstrated in 1960, but it was initially seen as a solution looking for a problem. "We thought it might have some communications and scientific uses, but we had no application in mind," recalled Arthur Schawlow, who won the Nobel Prize in Physics for his contributions to the invention of the laser. "If we had, it might have hampered us and not worked out as well." It was not until the development of ultratransparent fiber-optic cables in the early 1970s that it became clear how lasers could be used.

Finally, even when worthwhile ideas are recognized, it may require endless fussing with the little details to turn an idea into something really useful. One classic example is the bicycle, which was first invented in France in the 1790s. This early version, though, had no pedals, and couldn't be steered because the front wheel didn't turn. Over the next 100 years, a succession of small improvements was added, ranging from a steerable front wheel, to pedals, to the chain and sprocket arrangement for connecting the pedals to the back tire. It wasn't until the 1880s that something resembling the modern bicycle first appeared.

Sometimes the process of upgrading an innovation from joke to truly useful happens much faster. For example, when Apple Computers originally put its Newton Message Pad on the market in 1993, it helped create the category of the personal digital assistant (PDA). However, it was expensive, hard to use, and had handwriting recognition software whose failures became a national joke. The Newton never became a success.

When Palm Computing came out with the Palm Pilot in 1996–later changed to just Palm–it was cheaper, smaller, simpler, and easier to use. As a result, the Palm Pilot turned out to be much better suited to the marketplace.

THE SUPPLY OF IDEAS

How can we ensure that there are enough good ideas? One key is enough funding from governments and universities for research and development. Especially needed is basic research and early stage applied research, which is too uncertain and divorced from final applications to be financed by the financial markets, even today. The other key is having enough scientists and engineers to throw at new technologies. Once again, financing a scientific/engineering educational system requires government or university support. These are the seeds and the basic soil that new technologies grow in.

However, it need not strictly be funded by the U.S. government. Ideas and skilled people flow relatively easily across the national borders. No matter where the science is originally done, the U.S. high-performance financial market will attract a flow of ideas and trained people to the country. This is true even in an era of outsourcing.

One of the reasons to be optimistic about innovation is that the industrialized world has been devoting an increasing share of its resources to research and development. In the U.S., for example, nonfederal research and development reached 2 percent of GDP in 2002, its highest level ever. That's still not as high as it could be, but it's better than the roughly 1.5 percent at the beginning of the 1990s.

True, the performance of the federal government is not as strong. Government funding for energy and space R&D is down sharply as a share of GDP over the last 10 years. However, over the last couple of years the federal government has dramatically jumped its outlays for defense and health care R&D. And in November 2003, President George Bush signed a bill providing almost $4 billion in nanotechnology research funding over the next four years.

It's not simply a U.S. phenomenon. Despite Japan's economic woes, the share of GDP going to R&D in that country has actually risen over the last decade, from 2.6 percent in 1993 to more than 3.0 percent in 2001. Japanese companies such as NTT, Matsushita Electric, Sony, and Toyota have some of the biggest R&D budgets in the world. Overall, out of the top 20 global companies with the largest R&D outlays, only nine are American. Four are Japanese, and seven are European.

Then there's the rise of R&D spending in such fast-growing countries as Korea, Taiwan, China, and India. Between 1995 and 2001, Korea increased its R&D expenditures by more than 50 percent adjusted for inflation. That's despite being hit hard by the Asian financial crisis in 1997. According to the latest figures from the OECD, Korea now devotes about the same share of GDP to R&D as Japan and the U.S., and more than Germany, France, and the United Kingdom. That includes cutting-edge research at companies such as Samsung. Taiwan is following roughly the same rapid rate of increase as Korea. And Chinese R&D expenditures are now third in the world, behind only the U.S. and Japan.

The collective rise in R&D is beneficial to everyone, since ideas and innovations easily cross national boundaries. A U.S. company such as IBM may have research labs in Switzerland, China, India, Israel, and Tokyo, while Japanese companies such as Ricoh have research facilities in Silicon Valley. The big wave of drug company mergers in the 1990s created several U.S.-European hybrids, tied into both continents.

Such pooling of research is essential, because even a country as rich as the U.S. cannot afford to specialize in everything. The U.S. has the advantage in areas such as software and medical equipment, but overall one recent study showed that Europe leads in 12 scientific fields while the U.S. leads in only seven. The results were arrived at by measuring the number of papers published in leading scientific journals in key fields such as telecommunications.

THE GLOBAL EDUCATION BOOM

The global pool of educated workers is rapidly expanding as well, which is only a plus for innovation. For one thing, there has been a surge in the number of college-educated Americans. The percentage of people aged 25–29 with a college degree soared from 24.7 in 1995 to 29.3 in 2002. That's after being stuck at or below the 24 percent level since 1977.

TABLE 5: THE SPREAD OF COLLEGE EDUCATION

	PERCENTAGE OF AGE GROUP THAT HAS ATTAINED POST-SECONDARY EDUCATION (2001)			
	25–34	35–44	45–54	55–64
Canada	25	20	20	15
France	18	11	10	8
Germany	14	15	15	10
Italy	12	11	10	6
Japan	24	25	17	10
U.K.	21	18	18	12
U.S.	30	28	30	24

Source: OECD

All around the world, millions of young people are pouring out of the doors of institutions of higher learning. In the leading industrialized country, there's been a college boom, with the U.K., Canada, and Japan close to catching up with the U.S., in terms of the college education of the younger generation (see Table 5).

Human capital is being created at an accelerated rate in the less developed countries as well. China has ramped up the number of its college graduates in a very short period of time, going from about 1 million new graduates in 1998 to 2.1 million in 2003. The education boom has also become reality in countries such as India, Bangladesh, and Indonesia as well. In India, for example, the percentage of young people enrolled in higher education went from 6.6 in 1995 to 10.5 in 2000. That's a very big jump.

The biggest lack is the number of science and engineering doctoral students, especially in the U.S. The number of science and engineering doctorates awarded by universities in the U.S. has remained relatively flat for the last decade, with the number of Ph.D.s going to U.S. citizens actually falling by 12 percent since the mid-1990s. That's not good.

There may not be any way to completely remedy the science and engineering shortfall. However, it can certainly be ameliorated by boosting the amount of direct financial support for graduate students. The key, however, is to not tie the funding for students to particular fields of study or specific research grants by faculty members. Graduate students, especially in science and engineering, have to be allowed to seek out the hot or leading-edge areas of study, which may change very quickly. Giving grad students the flexibility to move among fields will benefit both them and the U.S. economy. Given the importance of technology for growth, it can't possibly be a waste.

IS THE BIOTECH REVOLUTION IMMINENT?

Keeping all this uncertainty at the top of our mind, it's time to take a closer look at the different technologies that could ignite the next round of growth. At the top of the list is biotech—the whole complex of genetic and technological solutions—which seems like it has the best chance of generating big winners in the near future. The underlying science has moved forward quickly since the sequencing of the human genome was announced in 2000.

There are enormous quantities of money being poured into every stage of the research development process by universities, venture capital firms, pharmaceutical companies, and the federal government. And there are plenty of companies that have products either in development or actually in clinical trials, promising therapies for everything from cancer to memory loss.

Disappointingly, biotech so far has not generated that one "killer app" that would ignite a revolution in health care. One reason, of course, is that the problem of creating new drugs and therapies may just be harder than scientists expected. Certainly there's a long list of companies with promising new drugs that turned out to be failures when tested on humans.

But looking deeper, there is another problem as well: Any biotech drug, to be truly successful, must meet two almost contradictory tests. It must save lots of lives, which would immediately create enormous demand for spending. But at the same time, to be really attractive to health care providers, it must cut health care costs as well.

Consider this contradiction more closely. The prime goal of any biotech product is to treat a disease or syndrome, and keep the patient alive longer. That's the only way it gets approved by the Food and Drug Administration (FDA), and that's what is going to drive demand. From this perspective, the biggest breakthrough product would be one that would completely cure some common form of cancer. That would create an enormous market for the drug. In other words, a successful drug, from the clinical point of view, is precisely one that would generate enormous demand for new spending.

To understand the magnitude of the cost, let's look at lung cancer, one of the most prevalent and deadly cancers, with over

150,000 new cases per year and a five-year survival rate of only 13 percent. Suppose that a biotech firm developed a successful treatment for lung cancer that kept patients alive for 10 additional years, at the cost of $10,000 per year. By itself, such a drug–which would be a major achievement–would eventually add $15 billion per year to the nation's health care bills.

In some cases success, by definition, will drive up health care costs. Consider, for example, the example of expensive biotech drugs used to treat chronic and debilitating conditions such as cystic fibrosis and multiple sclerosis. Such drugs may keep sufferers alive longer. But the longer they live, the more health care services they consume over the course of their lifetime, including expensive hospitalizations.

A simple, effective treatment for an illness–even a nonfatal one–will encourage more people to get treatment. Economists David Cutler and Mark McClellan, later to become head of the FDA, called this the "treatment expansion effect." They point out, for example, that diagnosis rates for depression doubled after drugs such as Prozac and Zoloft became available. So even if the use of drugs rather than psychotherapy was cheaper, the total medical bill for depression went up.

This is ghoulish stuff, but it helps explain why it has been so hard to come up with the breakthrough biotech drug. It has to satisfy two, not necessarily compatible, objectives. First, it would have to be successful treating an important disease, which would make it profitable for the company producing it. At the same time, the new drug would also have to reduce total health care spending.

In order to accomplish both objectives, it's likely that the breakthrough biotech drug will have to attack multiple diseases at once. That would produce high demand, while achieving the cost savings of replacing more than one existing therapy. For example, aspirin would have been the perfect candidate, since it's useful not only for pain relief, but approved for treating strokes, heart attacks, and arthritis as well. There's also evidence that it's effective against cancer and diabetes.

Unfortunately, it's not easy to find a drug that attacks multiple diseases, and that will pass through the regulatory system. This makes the bar for a successful biotech breakthrough a very high one indeed. It's likely going to happen–but the conditions to make it a true breakthrough will take longer to occur.

THE RETURN OF TELECOM

The second possible candidate for the Next Big Thing is the telecom. That may seem strange, given the massive overinvestment in the 1990s by telecom companies, both old and new. However, the mere fact of overinvestment in one decade doesn't preclude a new boom in the next. Consider the railroads in the late 19th century, for example. Overinvestment in locomotives, tracks, and freight cars helped create a near-depression in 1893–97. But the underlying demand for fast rail transportation was so strong that the industry bounced back within a couple of years after the downturn was over. The bust was followed by the so-called golden age of railroading, when passenger and freight miles soared, and so did income.

Telecom–which includes everything from wireless to cable to data networking to all sorts of new services–could very well follow the same pattern. The personal computer market seems to have matured, but underlying demand growth for telecom services has remained strong, especially in the wireless sector. Despite the telecom meltdown, the number of wireless subscribers rose by some 30 percent between 2000 and 2002.

Moreover, the overcapacity problem in telecom now seems to be a narrow rather than a broad one, focused mainly in long distance. Government data shows that the telecom "capital stock"– the installed base of communications equipment–is now back on its long-term growth path, after having gone through a bubble in the late 1990s. This suggests that if the economy recovers, any remaining overcapacity could be worked off.

That leaves the field open, potentially, for another round of the telecom revolution–one that is based on increasingly inexpensive wireless connectivity. It will become likely that all sorts of devices will be connected all the time, including your PDA, your computer, and various household appliances. At that point, a myriad of new applications will become possible that cannot be imagined right now.

As a candidate for the Next Big Thing, telecom has several advantages. The technology works, and is progressing rapidly. It doesn't have any big safety considerations to worry about, unless someone demonstrates conclusively that radio waves cause bodily harm. And there are certainly applications for all the new capabilities.

But there are two big hurdles that telecom faces. First is the uneven state of U.S. broadband access. Less than half of American households have high-speed access to the Internet. It may require some form of government subsidies or tax breaks to make broadband cheaper and more accessible, just as local roads and interstates were built with government funding.

The other problem is the ever-increasing hold of the large telecom companies on the market. The dominance of companies such as Verizon and Comcast, and their control over the local access, makes it that much harder for small start-ups to get a foothold. And as we will see in the next chapter, without the innovative energies that new firms bring to the party, the process of technological change goes much more slowly. That negates one of the main competitive advantages that the U.S. has.

THE ENERGY QUAGMIRE

In many ways, energy would be the logical area to find the next technological breakthrough. For one thing, energy innovations have been an absolutely critical part of every industrial revolution in the past. It is impossible to imagine our current society without electricity or the internal combustion engine.

More important, successful energy innovations have been sorely lacking over the last 100 years. The biggest breakthrough–nuclear power–worked in a technological sense, but it was a complete bust in terms of economics and safety. As a result, the main energy technologies that we use today–internal combustion for motor vehicles, fossil fuels for electricity production–would have been familiar to engineers in the early 1900s.

Our high-tech civilization could be derailed without a breakthrough in either energy distribution or generation. The big blackout of 2003 revealed the weaknesses of the electricity grid, as tech equipment consumes more and more power. And the prospect of continued global warming indicates the problems of relying on fossil fuels.

Thus, it should be a very good time for the high-performance financial markets to start funding energy start-ups. Unfortunately, the three main candidates for igniting an energy revolution–solar, hydrogen fuel cells, and nuclear–are either immature or extremely problematic. Hydrogen fuel cells improve the distribution and use of energy, nuclear power improves the generation of energy, and solar power improves both generation and distribution. Yet none of them leaps up as an immediate candidate for driving the next technological revolution without some dramatic improvement in economics and/or safety.

One big problem: Energy R&D has been lagging for quite a while, not just in the U.S. but around the world, as low oil prices took away the urgency. In real terms, global spending on energy R&D fell by an astounding 50 percent from its peak in 1980 through 1998, the last year available from the International Energy Agency. In the U.S., federal support for energy R&D declined by 64 percent from 1980 to 1997, in real terms, and then dropped by another 50 percent from 1997 to 2001. That helps explain why progress has been so slow in pushing energy technology forward. And private R&D spending at energy companies and utilities has not taken up the slack.

Take solar power, for example. The price of producing electricity from solar cells has been steadily dropping. However, even the most optimistic estimates suggest that a residential solar power installation produces electricity at roughly twice the cost of coal, taking all costs into account.

Proponents of solar power predict that the cost will be comparable with that of other sources of energy in a few years, perhaps as early as 2007. But there's where the unpredictability of innovation comes in. Such claims were made in the past, only to run into unforeseen problems. It turned out to be far harder, and far more costly, than anyone expected to make solar cells that efficiently turned sunlight into electricity. High-quality, high-purity silicon–which is the basis of the current generation of solar cells–is an expensive material. Moreover, except in a few sun-drenched locations, solar has to be supplemented with other energy sources.

That doesn't mean the problems can't be overcome–put it does mean that incremental innovation is not likely to produce a breakthrough technology that will radically transform the energy equation. The best hope for a "solar revolution" would be the success of one of the new technologies that are being tried in start-ups such as Nanosolar and Konarka, which rely on using lightweight conductive plastics rather than expensive silicon. But as we have seen, it's impossible to predict which new technologies will fail, which will succeed—and how long it will take.

The same thing is true for fuel cells and what is known as the "hydrogen economy." Where solar power addresses the energy-generation issue, fuel cells are related more to the question of distribution. Rather than using oil or gasoline as an energy source, fuel cells run on hydrogen, which generates far less damaging pollution. If the hydrogen could be produced cheaply and cleanly—a big if—a shift to fuel cells could dramatically reduce the carbon emissions that contribute to global warming.

However, even though fuel cells have been in use for decades—including being used in the Apollo space program—they may just turn out to be one of those innovations that take a long time to truly become commercial. Faced with problems such as weight, the safety of storing hydrogen, and the need for expensive materials, fuel cells are not yet ready to take the country by storm. According to a February 2003 report to Congress: "Absent other incentives, or a dramatic change in economics or availability of petroleum, the customer has very little reason to try an unproven new technology."

And finally, there's nuclear power. By all rights, nuclear power should have been one of the great innovations of the 20th century. All the right factors were in place. It was a brand-new technology, tapping into a completely different source of power than ever before. It had the potential to provide limitless power. And best of all, it worked.

After the first commercial nuclear power plant was opened in 1957, there was a tremendous amount of enthusiasm for nuclear power. Many liberals were enamored of the possibilities for progress from cheap energy. Consider, for example, the 1962 Port Huron statement, the founding document of the left-wing Students for a Democratic Society:

> Our monster cities, based historically on the need for mass labor, might now be humanized, broken into smaller communities, powered by nuclear energy, arranged according to community decision.

It's fair to say that if nuclear power had fulfilled its promise, then the economic history of the last 30 years would have been very different. When the oil price shock of the 1970s hit, gasoline prices would have still gone up. However, the U.S. would have had alternative, cheap sources of energy for other uses such as home heating and industrial power. It's very well possible that the productivity slowdown and stagnant economy of the 1970s would have been avoided, or at least ameliorated. Cheap energy would have boosted the economy tremendously.

But that's not what happened. Despite the oil price shock of 1973–which would naturally have increased the demand for nonoil fuels–orders for new nuclear plants dropped off after 1974, with none coming after 1978. And despite the soaring energy costs during the 1970s, and the need to put expensive pollution controls on coal- and oil-fired plants, the demand for nuclear power kept falling.

What happened? The utilities were aware, when they first started building nuclear power plants, that they were more expensive than the alternative sources of power. The expectation was that, as with other technologies, costs would fall as the utilities got more experience–but that's not what happened. As safety questions arose, the costs of construction increased until they were far greater than what was expected in the 1960s. As a result, nuclear power labors under an enormous cost disadvantage. A July 2003 report from MIT entitled "The Future of Nuclear Power" calculates that the cost of nuclear power is 6.7 cents per kilowatt hour, compared with 4.1 for gas and 4.2 for coal. That's not competitive by any stretch of the imagination.

The real question, then, is whether there are alternative designs for nuclear reactors that could allay safety concerns while lowering costs. In theory the answer is yes, and in theory such experimentation could be supported by the financial markets. Small-scale nuclear power plants based on alternative designs could be opened and tested fairly easily.

But for safety and security reasons, the sort of private-sector experimentation that drove the information technology revolution is impractical or even dangerous for testing new types of nuclear power plants. Especially these days, nuclear power has been criticized for being a potential source of fissionable material that terrorists could use to build atomic bombs. The MIT report advocates that the government should subsidize "a limited number of power plants that represent safety-enhancing evolutionary reactor design." This sort of government-run, incremental research program may eventually produce a safer, more economical nuclear reactor, but it will be a slow process.

NANOTECH ON THE HORIZON

Nanotechnology is a catchall phrase used to describe building up circuits and devices atom by atom. In actuality, it's used to refer to a whole range of different technologies, some of which are already in production, others which are working in the laboratory, and still others which are decades off.

Still, the list of future applications is long and getting longer:

for example, clothes made out of nanotubes, which are extremely strong and flexible; very sensitive sensors that can locate chemical and biological weapons; diagnostic tests that can detect cancer as early as possible; and nanorobots to deliver medication to precisely the right spots.

To a greater extent than any other technology, it's very hard to handicap how close nanotech really is to producing a breakthrough product or application. There have been plenty of demonstrations at the laboratory level of atom-by-atom manipulation. It's not obvious, though, what can be scaled up. The uncertainty factor is high—one of the products in the pipeline right now could turn out to be a big winner, or it could take decades.

The payoff from nanotech could be enormous, however. What's clear is that nanotechnology represents the next big breakthrough in manufacturing technology. The ability to make things atom by atom, conceivably by special order from each customer, would be a leap forward comparable to that of the assembly production line. Outside of semiconductors, the production technology in most of manufacturing—the assembly line—is a mature technology. Henry Ford could walk into a car assembly factory today and recognize it. In fact, because manufacturing production technology hasn't changed much, it's very easy to move factories overseas.

Nanotechnology could fundamentally change that equation. As manufacturing processes become much more sophisticated, it becomes harder to move them to other countries. Nanotech represents the best hope for keeping manufacturing-related jobs in the U.S.

EXPLOITATION OF SPACE

One of the biggest technological wild cards is the commercial exploitation of space. In many ways, space travel is as big an economic disappointment as nuclear power. In May 1961, President John F. Kennedy gave the famous speech in which he declared:

> This nation should commit itself to achieving the goal,
> before this decade is out, of landing a man on the moon and
> returning him safely to the earth.

In the years that followed, a substantial share of America's R&D resources were devoted to space travel. As noted in Chapter 4, space-related activities absorbed almost 60 percent of nondefense government R&D spending from 1962 to 1972. That commitment to space pulled resources away from other areas. As Kennedy noted in his speech:

> This decision demands a major national commitment of
> scientific and technical manpower, materiel and facilities,
> and the possibility of their diversion from other important
> activities where they are already thinly spread.

Unfortunately, despite succeeding in its main goal of putting a man on the moon, the space program has very few commercial spin-offs. According to NASA, the list of commercial spin-offs includes communications satellites, better mapping of forest fires, virtual reality, cordless drills, and ear thermometers.

But given the amount of money spent on space travel, the economic spin-offs should have been an order of magnitude greater to make it worthwhile. Space-related activities, instead of expanding, have become a smaller share of the economy over time. True, there was a momentary flurry of interest in space in the 1990s. A host of new space-based telecom systems were proposed, funded, and even implemented, with names like Iridium, Globalstar, Orbcomm, Teledesic, and more. Lou Dobbs left CNN's *Moneyline* show to become head of a new space-related dot-com, Space.com.

But the great satellite building boom of the late 1990s died an ignominious death. Iridium, Motorola's satellite-based communications system, was sold at a mere fraction of its cost. Globalstar, another satellite-based telecom system, filed for bankruptcy in 2002.

Nevertheless, space is still a potentially lucrative frontier, and space-related businesses could turn into the next breakthrough area if the cost of putting people or payloads into orbit can be reduced. That's the key technological choke point. Low-cost launch capabilities enable many more potential businesses to test out possible business models, including space tourism. And President George W. Bush's proposed manned mission to Mars, while not a commercial enterprise, has the potential of pumping more money into space R&D.

Right now space launches are still quite expensive. To put a small satellite into orbit costs $20 million or more. Several private companies now are trying to drive the launch cost down to half that cost or less. Much of the funding for these companies is coming from investors who made it big during the tech boom of the 1990s. For example, the main backer for SpaceX, one such company, is a person who made his fortune founding and selling PayPal, the online payment system, to eBay. Thus one technology breakthrough helps finance the next.

Once again, it is impossible to assess the odds of any of these companies being a commercial winner, even if they can successfully get a rocket into space. Added to the usual uncertainties is a military one: The government has kept a tight watch on space travel because of the defense implications.

PLAYING THE ODDS

Any of these technologies is a long shot to break through over the next five to 10 years. However, the fact that research is going on in all of these areas simultaneously raises the odds that at least one of them will become a big success. It's simple statistics.

More than that, the flexibility of the U.S. financial system means that any promising technology or product will get funding, even if it threatens existing companies. Once any of these technologies gets closer, the resources will be there, and that will accelerate its economic impact.

CHAPTER 7

Why Finance Matters

Because of their role in financing new ideas, financial markets keep alive the process of "creative destruction"–whereby old ideas and organizations are constantly challenged and replaced by new, better ones. Without vibrant, innovative financial markets, economies would invariably ossify and decline.

Raghuram G. Rajan and Luigi Zingales
Saving Capitalism from the Capitalists

The stock market boom of the 1990s has been tarnished and cursed as a "bubble." The tech and telecom bust, the corruption on Wall Street and at the mutual funds, the corporate accounting scandals–all have combined to undercut the global reputation of the U.S. financial markets.

Yet ultimately the case for rational exuberance rests on the superior ability of the U.S. financial system to fund innovation, as it did in the 1990s. Scientific creativity is essential, and so is spending on research and development and an educated workforce. But at the end of the day, the crucial difference between cautious and exuberant growth is as much financial as technological.

Then, if and when any of the new technologies described in the previous chapter shows promise, the money is available–in staggering amounts–to bring it to market, and to create new products, new companies, and new industries. Institutional and individual investors are able to shift their resources very quickly from one sector to another, like a mobile army, able to overwhelm the enemies of growth just as they did in the 1990s.

Finance plus technology is stronger than either one alone. By combining the two, we greatly increase the odds of not just one technological revolution but a series of them. The end result is to accelerate change and encourage exuberant growth. That, in turns, feeds back into the booming stock market, which encourages yet more investment in innovative companies.

That's what economist Robert Shiller missed in his 2000 book, *Irrational Exuberance*. For Shiller, the stock market was all about feedback loops, the "self-fulfilling psychology of a roaring stock market" and what he called "naturally occurring Ponzi processes." In other words, investors could systematically fool themselves, and drive the market up.

But Shiller downplayed the possibility that the exuberance could itself have a positive impact, by helping increase the speed of technological change. It is the power of the financial markets and new technology together that allows us to be optimistic about the future.

INNOVATION AND FINANCIAL MARKETS

Here's a statement that should be obvious to everyone, but isn't: Financial systems matter. The way an economy allocates capital can have an enormous effect on its performance, both in the short term and in the long term.

For example, an authoritarian system allocates funds from the top down. Such systems are very good for getting certain types of large-scale projects built, such as roadways and other infrastructure projects. The Soviet Union, of course, was a classic authoritarian financial system, as in some ways is China.

However, authoritarian systems don't even try to allocate funds efficiently, or to the most profitable uses. As a result, there's a lot of waste—roads that go nowhere, buildings that no one wants to occupy. Moreover, there's no room for funding innovation, which by definition doesn't fit into any preconceived plan.

The question of how innovation gets financed is critical. Simply put, it's difficult to fund the research and development of new technologies that challenge the status quo. That's especially true in a mature economy like the U.S., where most of the economic niches are filled with big players ready to defend their turf. Small companies are more likely to be willing to run with big new ideas—but that requires them to be able to tap into the financial markets.

Starting up a new business is very expensive. The earliest stages—when someone is working alone in a garage or in a laboratory to see if an idea has promise—can be done on the cheap. But once a company starts to grow beyond a few people, it begins to consume money very quickly. It needs engineers to develop and figure out how to manufacture the product. It needs a sales staff to get potential customers to even consider buying the product. They all have to be compensated before the company starts earning any revenues. For example, if a start-up hires 10 people, at $100,000 per year, that's a million dollars right off the bat annually, even without paying for real estate, computers, or anything else.

Where will the money come from? Friends and family, perhaps, or from local wealthy investors—"angels," in the parlance. While that works for some people, such sources of funds are hit-or-miss.

And most financial institutions are unwilling to touch start-ups. With a high risk of failure and no collateral, a new company is a bad bet for a bank loan. With no cash flow, it's nearly impossible for a start-up to sell bonds. And major equity markets are not open to the newest companies. Both the Nasdaq and the New York Stock Exchange have various requirements to be listed, but both of them require that a company have a minimum of assets or profits—that is, it must have raised some money already in the past.

HIGH-PERFORMANCE FINANCIAL MARKETS

Over time, the U.S. has developed a solution to the problem of how to fund and promote innovation in a mature economy. It does not happen automatically—instead, it requires what we will call a *high-performance financial market.* Such a market includes some key financial instruments for financing innovative activity—notably venture capital (VC), stock options, and high-yield or "junk" bonds—that are far better developed in the U.S. than in any other country.

VC is a way to fund high-risk enterprises, based on new ideas and brainpower. Stock options turn employees of innovative companies into investors, by allowing them to accept lower wages now in exchange for the possibility of future gains. And junk bonds specialize in funding risky but potentially lucrative physical investments, such as telecom infrastructure.

Let's start with VC. VC, as a way of financing start-ups, is a uniquely American invention, going back to 1946 and a Boston-based firm called American Research and Development. For years, venture capital occupied only a small corner of the financial markets, but in the 1990s it became much more important. In 1995, venture investments totaled $7.7 billion, rising to a stunning $106 billion in 2000, before falling back to a $17 billion annual rate in the first three quarters of 2003. Still, that amounted to almost 8 percent of corporate borrowing–with the share sure to rise as the tech sector recovers and venture investment accelerates again.

Moreover, companies backed by venture capital are very important to the economy. At the end of 2000, fully 20 percent of all public firms had been financed in part by venture capital. Such venture-backed companies account for 11 percent of total sales, and at that point, about one-third the value of public firms. That's according to Paul Gompers and Josh Lerner's encyclopedic study of venture capital, *The Money of Invention.*

How does venture capital deal with the problem of financing innovation? Venture capital firms are limited partnerships that funnel money from pension funds, large corporations, universities, and the like into new and innovative businesses. The VC firms get a percentage of the money invested, but their really big payoff comes if the company goes public, or if it gets sold to a bigger company.

On the one hand, this arrangement gives venture capitalists an incentive to be greedy, self-centered, and mercenary. They will do anything to get a company to the point where it can be sold off, even if it requires replacing the founding entrepreneur with a professional manager. That happens with some regularity, often leaving the founder with little stake in the company and a heartfelt disgust for venture capitalists.

But the flip side is that the only way that venture capitalists score a big win is by helping create a new company that is valuable to someone else—either to investors, by way of an IPO, or to a larger company. That makes venture capital unique in financial history. No other institution—ever—was devoted exclusively to assessing and funding innovation for pure profit motives. Unlike big companies, venture capitalists have no existing products or markets to protect. And unlike governments, venture capitalists don't have to worry about lobbyists or the need to favor local companies.

Venture capitalists are the equivalent of economic subversives. They have no vested interest in the status quo, and they do spectacularly well during periods of exuberant growth. So far they are the best answer to the question of how to fund innovative small businesses.

Of course, many of those new businesses may turn out to be complete and abject failures. Some of them may be so absurd that investors look back afterward and ask, "How could I have ever been so stupid to think that Pets.com would be the next Microsoft?" In fact, a list of failed dot-coms makes one appreciate the sheer imagination that must have gone into dreaming up businesses that had no chance at all of succeeding.

Nevertheless, VC-backed start-ups do a lot better, on average, than ones without VC. "Ninety percent of new entrepreneurial businesses that don't attract venture capital fail within three years," Gompers and Lerner report. By comparison, the failure rate for VC-backed companies is roughly one-third.

Venture funding is better than any other type of finance in funneling money into innovation. Part of the reason is that venture investment is not simply a one-time allocation of funds. Instead, it goes in stages. In the early stage, a venture fund will put money into a lot of different start-ups at once, without really being able to determine which ones will succeed and which ones won't. But it will be just enough money to get the companies started.

Then, when the start-ups come back for the next round of

funding, the venture capitalists only allocate money to the potential winners, while the losers fall by the wayside. Because of this staged and hands-on approach, money invested through VC funds has a higher chance of going to something technologically innovative. As a result, a dollar of VC seems to stimulate three times as many patents as the same amount of corporate R&D.

STOCK OPTIONS

Start-ups also get part of their financing by issuing stock options to their employees. That is, the employees accept lower salaries, in exchange for options that give them the chance to buy company stock at a low price in the future. In effect, stock options turn workers into investors–they put their salary reductions into the company, and they get to share in any gains from successful innovation.

The use of options is absolutely essential for start-ups. It gives them a chance to attract high-quality workers looking for a big score. It motivates employees, since the only way they win big is if the company succeeds. And it aligns the interests of workers with the venture capitalists and other outside investors.

The big debate today is over how to account for stock options. Accounting purists argue that grants of stock options are clearly compensation to workers, and they should be valued as such and deducted from current income (which they have not been). In the language of accounting, they should be "expensed." Meanwhile, many top executives from Silicon Valley say that forcing them to deduct the value of stock options from their income will make it harder for them to offer stock options, and make them less competitive.

What makes the debate tricky is that stock options in a large corporation actually serve a very different purpose than stock options in start-ups and tech companies in general. At a start-up, it makes sense to view an employee who gives up some salary and accepts stock options as an investor, since he or she is putting in money (in the form of forgone salary) and taking exactly the same risk as an outside investor. In effect, a grant of a stock option at a start-up is an equity transaction, making the worker a type of partner. From that perspective, treating the stock option as labor compensation would be wrong.

The same rationale, though somewhat weaker, applies at larger tech companies as well. Tech companies need to keep up a rapid rate of innovation in order to compete. That may require employees to put in a lot of unpaid extra hours. In effect, these extra hours are investments adding to the company's intellectual capital, which would show up as such if companies recorded intellectual capital on their balance sheets the same way that they do physical capital. The stock options are offered to keep workers investing in the company's intellectual capital and future innovations, and to give them a share in the gains from those innovations.

Consider, by contrast, a top executive at an existing company that is not on the leading edge of innovation. A stock option grant to such an executive has much more of the quality of labor compensation, and should be treated that way.

As a result, no single rule fits. From the perspective of encouraging exuberant growth, it makes sense to encourage stock options at companies that are following a strategy of trying to innovate. On the other hand, from the perspective of good accounting, it makes sense to treat stock options at less-innovative companies as labor compensation. The appropriate compromise may be to require companies to deduct the value of stock options from the company's earnings, but only for top officers of companies over a certain size. That will eliminate CEO abuses, without destroying the ability of tech firms and start-ups to use options as they need to.

JUNK BONDS

Another type of financial instrument essential for a high-performance financial market is high-yield securities, also known as junk bonds. These high-yield securities are available to fund businesses, such as telecom start-ups, which have collateral–the physical networks–but very uncertain prospects.

Even newer than venture capital, junk bonds were popularized by Michael Milken of Drexel Burnham Lambert in the 1980s. His idea was that, properly priced, bonds could be sold to fund business ventures, even if there was a measurable risk that the bonds wouldn't get paid back.

Junk bonds got a bad reputation because they were used to fund leveraged buyouts, including the RJR Nabisco deal that was the subject of the 1990 book *Barbarians at the Gate* by Bryan Burrough and John Helyar. Such uses of junk bonds appeared to add little to economic productivity. In fact, junk bonds were derided as just another way of cheating investors and making the financial system more unstable. When Milken served two years in prison in the early 1990s for violations of securities law, junk bonds were discredited even further.

But junk bonds were also used by companies such as MCI to build a telecom network to challenge AT&T. It turned out in the 1990s that high-yield bonds were the perfect financial instrument to build cable and telecom networks. These networks were too expensive to be funded by VC directly, but because there was a physical asset–the network–it was easy to sell bonds. Thus, high-yield bonds financed much of the telecom boom of the 1990s.

FINANCE AS COMPETITIVE EDGE

It's the presence of financial instruments such as VC and high-yield bonds that helps fuel exuberant growth in the U.S. By comparison, the European financial markets are way behind the U.S. when it comes to these high-risk markets. The European high-yield market is only about one-tenth the size of that of the U.S., while VC in Europe is much smaller as well. In 2002, there were 9.8 billion euros in VC funding in Europe, roughly about 45 percent of the U.S. total.

Germany, Great Britain, and Japan tried for decades to develop venture capital industries, with little success. For example, German banks started VC funds as far back as the 1960s, but they were far too conservative and did not invest in small, innovative firms. Similarly, there was a wave of British VC firms in the late 1970s and early 1980s, but they ended up focusing on management buyouts of existing firms, with little money put toward start-ups.

That is not to say that companies in Europe and Japan don't have access to capital. France, Germany, and Japan all have much higher savings rates than the U.S. And banks in Europe and Japan have historically been much more willing to lend than the ones in the U.S.

But while there's a high level of savings in Europe and Japan, the financial institutions don't exist to funnel it in the right way. The bank-based financial systems in Germany and Japan are based on relationships between lenders and big borrowers, a weaving together of interests. Thus, Deutsche Bank is the largest single shareholder of Daimler Chrysler, with 12 percent of the outstanding shares. But such relationships—which work well during times of cautious growth—make it much harder for the financial system to move funds to new companies in rapidly growing innovative sectors.

The ability to raise money for new ideas is a key reason why the U.S. was able to run ahead of Europe and Japan during the decade of the 1990s, and even today. Remember that Japanese and European companies have had access to fundamentally the same technology as the U.S.–after all, Intel gets more than half its revenues from overseas, and the Internet is global. It was finance that made the difference–without the money from the financial sector, the Information Revolution in the U.S. would have proceeded much more slowly, as it did in Europe and Japan.

GOVERNMENT AND INNOVATION

Can government funding take the place of VC? Certainly the government plays a key role when it comes to stimulating exuberant growth. The federal government has to take responsibility for funding basic scientific research, and early stage applied research that is far from commercialization. Moreover, the need to provide as much funding as possible for scientific education is purely the province of government, since it benefits all companies equally.

But it's a mistake to ask government bureaucrats and politicians to get involved in the actual development of new products. They are not motivated by the idea of finding the most profitable technology, or the technology that will excite people and open up new possibilities.

Instead, government decisions are by definition more sensitive to political pressures and lobbying. That means technology decisions will be made for the wrong reasons, including protecting jobs in the districts of key politicians. Big companies that can make big political contributions are protected and aided.

Given the nature of politics, it's also hard for the government to cut off money from ventures that aren't working. For example, the synfuel program, started during the Carter administration, gives tax credits to companies that produce synthetic fuel from coal. At the time when the bill was originally passed, in 1980, it wasn't a bad experiment to see what could be done to cut the nation's dependence on foreign oil. Today, it's generally agreed that synthetic fuel contributes little to the country's energy supply. Yet with the aid of intense industry lobbying, the credits persist, costing taxpayers billions each year.

LARGE CORPORATIONS AND INNOVATION

Big companies can be very good at incremental research, which either improves existing product lines or extends them to new customers. However, it's far more difficult for a big company to handle disruptive innovations that undercut its existing products, or take it into new areas where it doesn't have expertise.

The twin management notions of outsourcing and core competencies can help blind corporate managers to cutting-edge innovations. The idea of core competencies encourages a corporation to identify the things that it does well, and focus on them. Outsourcing of course, is a way of saving money or resources by farming out tasks to other, more specialized companies.

In theory, such focus on a few key markets or products should make it easier for a corporation to be innovative, since managers won't have to worry about extraneous matters. In practice, however, corporate managers will still have a vested interest in the status quo or in their existing products and markets. After all, they, along with plenty of other people in the same company, built their careers on existing products. Supporting a product that eats away at a company's existing markets can be the equivalent of committing career suicide.

In a world of certainty, that attitude works quite well: Companies just plow straight ahead, spending money on research or developing new products based on things they already know how to do. There are no surprises, nothing unexpected–the companies know in what direction they are heading. In other words, the "technology landscape" is well mapped out and well understood, and getting to the future is just a matter of spending enough time and enough money.

But as the technology landscape becomes more uncertain, big companies have less of an edge. There's a reason why the first online stores were opened by companies that didn't have a vested interest in maintaining the profitability of their bricks and mortars. Only after the competition came into being did the big companies leap onto the Internet bandwagon.

Conversely, whenever they can, existing large companies will try to exercise financial and political clout to make life difficult for new entrants. For example, regulations in most states make it very difficult to sell cars over the Internet without the assistance of an existing motor vehicle dealership.

That is even more of a problem in Europe and Japan. In Europe, innovation has been slowed by opposition from entrenched corporations, which have mustered the political force to maintain the status quo. For example, even today retailers in European countries such as Germany operate under tight zoning and labor laws, while retail discounting and promotions are often restricted as well, in part to protect makers of brand-name merchandise. But limiting competition has the unforeseen consequence of slowing technological change in retailing.

For example, the most technologically progressive retailer in the U.S. was giant discounter Wal-Mart, which used computers to cut costs, to link with suppliers, and to generally run the most efficient and profitable operation in retailing. The pressure from Wal-Mart forced the rest of the retailing industry to invest in technology, or become history. A 2001 report on productivity from the McKinsey Global Institute observed:

> In general merchandise . . . we found that Wal-Mart directly and indirectly caused the bulk of the productivity acceleration through ongoing managerial innovation that increased competitive intensity and drove the diffusion of best practice (both managerial and technological).

Without the pressure from Wal-Mart and from other innovative retailers, productivity gains in retailing in France and Germany were much slower than in the U.S.

DRAWING IN IDEAS AND PEOPLE

When it comes to global competition, finance is the trump card. Foreign investors are putting $600 billion to $700 billion annually into U.S. financial assets, in large part because investments promise higher returns in the U.S. than the rest of the world. And that, in part, is because the U.S. financial system is better at allocating capital than its competitors. The ability to raise money and lend it out to the right places is a competitive edge, especially in a fast-changing world.

But it's not just money that is drawn in by the strength of the U.S. financial markets–it's smart people and good ideas as well. Because of the high-powered financial markets here, it's easier to get financing for innovation, which attracts entrepreneurs from elsewhere. Hotmail, the first free Web-based email system, was started in 1996 by Sabeer Bhatia, who grew up in Bangalore, India (Hotmail was bought by Microsoft for $400 million in 1997). Similarly, Silicon Valley turned into a mecca for ambitious and smart engineers and programmers from India, China, and elsewhere.

As this book is written, in late 2003, the lure of the U.S. financial advantage doesn't look quite so strong. China and India are in the full flush of their boom periods, and there's plenty of money available there. Meanwhile, venture capitalists in the U.S. are still recovering from the tech bust, and the initial public offering markets have not yet opened up.

But as we'll see in the next chapter, the U.S. financial markets are more mature and resilient. The Chinese financial system, and to a lesser degree the Indian financial system, are vulnerable to shocks. Over the medium run, it will turn out that it will be much easier to get financing for risky innovative ventures in the U.S.

EMBRACING OPTIMISM

No one can guarantee a new technological breakthrough will happen next year, or the year after, or the year after that. There are plenty of promising innovations out there, but there's no way to tell which one is going to come to fruition. The Internet cannot be repeated on command.

But one thing is certainly true: The chances of something good happening go up when there's enough money to explore all of the different alternatives. Think of the U.S. financial system as a growth medium, a rich nutrient solution able to provide nourishment to innovation. That makes it more likely that exuberant growth will bloom in the future.

CHAPTER 8

The Advantages and Disadvantages of Bubbles

Innovation is a highly risky business. As a result, any financial system that aggressively funds cutting-edge technologies is going to be more prone to booms and busts.

Think of it this way. As each potential new technology breakthrough comes onto the scene, investors leap in with the goal of getting a piece of the Next Big Thing. This quickly drives up stock prices, until the actual usefulness of the innovation becomes clear. Then stock prices either collapse (the more likely possibility) or continue to rise.

In effect, a high-performance financial system is actually likely to induce a series of bubbles, each one corresponding to a different technology. The telecom bubble may be followed by a biotech bubble, or a fuel cell bubble, or a space bubble. We shall call this a *pulsating market*.

This behavior is both a feature and a bug (to use the language of programmers). On the one hand, volatility is the hallmark of a financial market in which investors are willing to put their money into high-risk, high-return innovations that sometimes succeed and sometimes fail. Alternating periods where it is easy to raise money with periods of tight credit may also be a good stimulus to innovation.

But such a financial system may violate the traditional economic precepts of efficiency and stability. Much of the funding may be wasted on technological dead ends and innovations that don't pan out. Worse, every time a bubble bursts, there's a chance that something unexpected will happen, and the bust will turn into a full-fledged financial crisis. Nobody wants to see a repeat of the Asian financial crisis, or the Japanese bank crisis, where bank lending and financial markets freeze up.

That's why a high-performance financial system will only work in a country such as the U.S., which combines financial strength with a strong central bank. The banks and other financial institutions have to be well diversified and well funded. Moreover, there has to be a central bank with the means and will to back up the financial system, with a political system willing to make reforms when things are tough.

Over the last few years, the U.S. financial markets have proven themselves to be robust and resilient, having survived the triple punch of 2001–the end of the stock market boom, the Enron debacle, and the terrorists attacks. Certainly there was some damage–venture capital (VC) funding fell way off, and there were some high-profile bankruptcies, including Enron and Worldcom. But overall, financial disruptions were hardly apparent: nonfinancial corporations were easily able to raise a total of almost $500 billion through the bond market in 2001 and 2002, mortgage lending hit record levels, and consumers with good records had no trouble getting all the credit that they wanted. In 2001 and 2002, household mortgage debt increased by more than 20 percent, and consumer credit rose by about 12 percent.

From this perspective, the vulnerable spot of the Chinese and Indian economies may lie not in their manufacturing prowess or the skills of their workforce, but in the weaknesses of the financial systems. In a capitalist economy, financial crises are a fact of life–and we don't know yet whether Chinese and Indian financial and political systems are strong enough to stand the stress.

THE BANE OF BUSTS

The nature of financial systems is that they are prone to booms and busts. Financial markets operate on the basis of trust–investors put their money into stock certificates, pieces of paper, and trust that they will get it back, and more. Lenders give their money to borrowers based on optimism about the future, which can evaporate overnight.

Financial crises can come in all sorts of forms: stock market crashes, bank runs, currency crisises. They all have one basic characteristic: Investors lose their trust in an asset or security, leading to selling, which feeds on itself. In his classic book *Manias, Panics, and Crashes,* economic historian Charles Kindleberger wrote:

> Expectations can be quickly altered. Something, sometimes almost nothing, causes a shadow to fall on credit, reverses expectations, and the rush for liquidity is on . . . The system is one of positive feedback. A fall in prices reduces the value of collateral and induces banks to call loans or refuse new ones, causing merchant houses to sell commodities,

households to sell securities, industry to postpone
borrowing, and prices to fall still further.

In particular, a boom sustained by investment in new technologies has a good chance of ending in a sharp downturn, simply
because the technology uncertainty is always high. Alvin Hansen,
mentioned earlier as a leading American economist during the
1930s and 1940s, noted:

> Investment must often be made on a daring hunch which
> may or may not work out. Much investment is the result
> of waves of optimism produced by boom conditions. It
> cannot be justified on the basis of close and cautious
> calculations. . . . The investment demand schedule toward
> the end of a boom may look silly in the cold aftermath
> when bitter realities must be faced . . . mass optimism
> may rapidly develop into mass pessimism.

The damage can spread throughout the entire financial system, as financial firms are left holding bad debts, assets without
any value, and collateral no longer worth the paper it is printed on.
Confidence dries up, and in the worst cases paralyzes the financial
system, which depends on a web of trust. That's what happened in
Japan in the 1990s—after the real estate bubble of the 1980s burst,
it made such a mess of the banking system that the economy had
not recovered more than a decade later.

AVOIDING THE BOOM, AVOIDING THE BUST?

The history of financial regulation—including the creation of the
Federal Reserve Bank—can be interpreted as a series of attempts to

understand how to avoid financial crises, or if they happen, to minimize the damage. There's a consensus that when a crisis occurs, the main obligation of the central bank is to provide liquidity to the financial system—that is, to make enough cheap funds available to banks and other financial institutions that they are not forced to foreclose on their borrowers.

But there's far less agreement about whether the central bank has an obligation to try to choke off financial booms before they get out of control. Federal Reserve chairman Alan Greenspan has argued, repeatedly, that it would have been wrong to preemptively raise rates to deflate the boom of the 1990s:

> ... nothing short of a sharp increase in short-term rates
> that engenders a significant economic retrenchment is
> sufficient to check a nascent bubble. The notion that
> a well-timed incremental tightening could have been
> calibrated to prevent the late 1990s bubble is almost
> surely an illusion.

On the other side, there are those economists, such as Stephen Cecchetti, former research director for the New York Fed, who believe it was obvious that the stock market was overpriced, and that the Fed should have acted sooner. Writes Cecchetti:

> Central bankers should not willfully ignore developments
> in asset markets when there is a reasonable chance that
> they will create gross distortions in the investment and
> consumption decisions.

One of Cecchetti's central points is that the bubble allowed firms to waste money, because financing was too cheap.

For firms, it becomes too easy to obtain financing. . . .
It is not much of a challenge to find examples of internet
companies that were able to raise staggering sums of
money in equity markets, only to crash and burn several
years later. The funds they used could clearly have been
better invested elsewhere.

The clear implication is that an objective observer in 1999 and 2000 could have easily identified the companies that should never have received funding.

ADVANTAGES OF PULSATING MARKETS

However, as we saw in Chapter 6, innovation is profoundly unpredictable. It's easy to make value judgments after the fact, but at the time, it's very hard to distinguish ridiculous investments from ones that turn out to be eminently successful. For example, when Google was founded in 1998, very few people would have believed that the world needed another Web search engine, given how many were already in existence. But the Google technology turned out to be far superior.

Visualize that the technology landscape is extremely rugged and craggy, like the Scottish highlands. We could be in a valley, and not have any idea what's happening over the next hill, or the one after that. Similarly, if we want to find the Next Big Thing, there's no way of telling which technological direction is going to be the most fruitful to explore.

As a result, to discover and develop the best new technologies, it may be helpful for policymakers to allow financial booms and busts—that is, periods of cheap capital and exuberance that alternate with periods of expensive capital and tight money. The periods of easy money feed the exploration and exuberance. Start-ups strike out into new territories, creating excitement and new opportunities. The access to cheap capital enables people to try a lot of things that wouldn't be possible otherwise. There's a gold rush mentality–any news of success draws in more money to fund more explorations.

This perspective gives us another way to think about the last 10 years. The conventional wisdom is that the period of exuberance during the boom period–especially 1999 and 2000–was a bubble. This word–which doesn't have a good formal definition–is a loaded term. It carries connotations of something fragile, which was never quite real in the first place.

But rather than a bubble, the second half of the 1990s could just as easily be called an "age of exploration." The low cost of capital enabled adventuresome people and companies to try out lots of new ideas simultaneously, and on a large enough scale that they got a fair test.

Thus, the U.S. financial market funded a lot of search parties to explore the technology landscape surrounding the Internet, which turned out to be much more complicated than anyone expected. Surefire winners such as Netscape ended up as mere bookkeeping entries on Time Warner's books. Some seemingly attractive big bets–Webvan, for example, the online grocery business–simply failed. Other companies, which first seemed spectacular successes, and then seemed ready to go under–Amazon.com, for example– are going to be quite prosperous businesses. Meanwhile, some companies, such as eBay, are big winners in niches that no rational planner could have predicted.

The boom phase is inevitably followed by a bust–but that has a real purpose as well. When capital gets expensive, that serves as an effective screening device for separating the successful innovations from the wanna-bes. It is survival of the fittest, but according to a very specific rule. The companies that are self-supporting–that is, profitable–survive. The ones that are still dependent on outside funds die.

Despite all the waste and corruption, and despite all the companies that went under, the U.S. ultimately benefited from the period of cheap financing in the 1990s. What the U.S. had that its competitors did not was a financial system that rewarded innovation. Certainly it was not perfect–there was plenty of corruption. Nevertheless, such a financial system is the greatest competitive weapon that a country can have.

CAN THE PULSATING MARKETS BE COPIED?

Can other countries duplicate the U.S. financial system? Eventually, but to copy the U.S. financial structure is far more complicated than copying a computer program or a router. It's not just a matter of giving out money during the boom–equally important is whether the financial markets are able to absorb the stress of the bust when it inevitably comes.

The U.S. financial markets have several advantages that make booms and busts easier to handle than ever before. First, U.S. financial markets are simply bigger and deeper than anywhere else. As of November 2003, the total capitalization of the U.S. stock markets was in excess of $13 trillion. The next closest, the Tokyo exchange, was less than $3 trillion, measured at current exchange rates. That means a bet that would dwarf most financial markets simply doesn't make a ripple in the U.S.

Related to that, the U.S. has the advantage of the biggest and most diverse economy in history. That means even big risks can be absorbed more easily. By contrast, most large economies are far more concentrated in a few key industries. For example, when the financial crisis hit Japan in 1990, it was heavily dependent on manufacturing, with almost 25 percent of the nonagricultural workforce in the factory sector. By contrast, only 13 percent of U.S. workers were in manufacturing in 2000. This kind of diversification is actually a big advantage.

But it's more than just size. The U.S. financial markets have also embraced the principle of securitization, which spreads the risk around. For example, after banks lend money to home buyers for mortgages, the risk of the loan is spread around by bundling a set of mortgages together, and repackaging them as mortgage-backed securities. The same thing is done for credit card and auto loans. In theory, it should be possible to distribute the risks widely enough to guard against even the biggest busts. Loans can be split into a lot of different pieces; investments can be hedged; futures markets or derivatives can be used to guard against the possibilities of big price movements. Thus, no single bank or investor had enough Enron or WorldCom bonds to trigger a problem.

Finally, and perhaps most important, the U.S. has a strong central bank. Led by Chairman Alan Greenspan, the Federal Reserve started cutting interest rates aggressively in early 2001. That made it easier for banks and companies to clean up their balance sheets. Any short-term debt–potentially risky because it could be cut off at any moment–could be refinanced with safer long-term debt at low interest rates. The amount of short-term commercial paper issued by nonfinancial businesses fell by $150 billion between the end of 2000 and the end of 2002.

Similarly, consumers could start the process of refinancing their mortgages at lower interest rates. By the time that the Enron scandal broke over the summer and fall of 2001 and the terrorist attack shook the financial markets, the economy was much better prepared. There is no substitute for effective policy.

The net result is that the U.S. financial markets seem to be less susceptible to the cascading effects of defaults or of technology-related busts. No one is saying that they are invulnerable—the collapse of hedge fund Long-Term Capital Management in 1998 certainly had the potential to do deep damage, and there is always the lurking fear that a large financial institution could take stupid risks, knowingly or unknowingly. But the ability of the U.S. financial system to shake off the telecom and tech busts is good news for the future.

GOVERNANCE PROBLEMS

It's not just the central bank—a financial crisis tests the entire political system. It's often necessary to make tough choices, to impose sacrifices on one sector of the economy to help bail out another. For example, to solve the savings and loan crisis in the 1980s, Congress had to empower the Resolution Trust Corporation to close or consolidate scores of politically influential banks, and give it authority to spend the money necessary to do so—at the time, estimated to be in the hundreds of billions of dollars—to cover all the liabilities (in the end, the net cost to the public of cleaning up the mess was roughly $80–90 billion).

By contrast, the Japanese political system was unable to react to a banking system essentially paralyzed by bad debt after the stock and real estate market crashes of the early 1990s. To preserve its own political base, the ruling Liberal Democratic Party effectively blocked the financial and regulatory reforms that would be necessary to transform the economy. The result was to preserve the status quo that enabled them to stay in power, at the cost of accepting a decade of stagnation.

If and when a financial crisis comes in China, no one knows whether the political system will end up performing more like the

U.S. (quarrelsome but ultimately effective) or more like the Japanese (ultimately ineffective). As this book is being written, signs of a potential financial problem are in place. The Chinese money supply is growing at an astonishing 20 percent per year, showing an amazing amount of money being poured into the economy to pump up the boom. What's more, the money is mainly going to finance not innovation, but a mammoth wave of construction, with factories and office buildings springing up everywhere.

The danger is that the Chinese government will not be able to act effectively in the event of a financial crisis. It will have to bail out banks and companies that are overextended, while forcing needed consolidation at the same time, even of enterprises that are politically connected to the Chinese leadership. A quick resolution may or may not prove difficult, depending on political realities.

POLITICS AND FINANCE

Technology is fueled by finance, which in turn is linked to politics. All three–technology, finance, politics–are necessary to reap the innovative benefits of a pulsating market. Without the boom-era easy financing, it's harder for new innovative companies to get funding. And without the intervention of the central bank and the political system, financial markets can get out of control, especially on the downside.

Indeed, getting the political system on the side of exuberant growth is essential. But it is not easy–and that is the subject of the next chapter.

CHAPTER 9

Building a Coalition for Exuberant Growth

The biggest threat to exuberant growth today is the lack of popular support for innovation. The enemies of exuberant growth are just as numerous and diverse as they have ever been. And the obvious supporters of exuberance–the beneficiaries of the 1990s–are feeling beaten down and woebegone.

The stock market has doubled since 1993, but investors still feel betrayed by scandal after scandal, with the mutual funds just the latest example of corruption. Managerial salaries are up 16 percent, in real terms, over that stretch, but educated workers are worried that their jobs are being shipped out to India and China. And the poverty rate is down from 1993, but workers with only a high school diploma are struggling with steep unemployment rates and big layoffs.

The result is a deepening cynicism about growth. After all,

who needs another boom if the gains are just going to be stolen by corrupt companies and managers? Who needs another technology growth spurt if the end result is just going to be more layoffs?

These feelings eat away at the popular support for pro-growth policies. Government R&D spending, outside of defense and health, has stagnated. Support for the education and training of scientists and engineers is not what it should be. And the biggest U.S. competitive advantage—its ability to finance innovation through venture capital and stock options—has come under severe assault from Congress and from the Financial Accounting Standards Board (FASB), which wants to make it much more costly to issue stock options.

That's why the fear and distrust of innovation and exuberant growth must be addressed very directly. Historically there has been a real split between politicians who advocated pro-growth policies and those politicians who focused on economic security and fairness concerns. In broad terms, Republicans today have positioned themselves as the pro-growth party of tax cuts, while Democrats have mostly tried to address inequality and unfairness.

Yet pro-growth and pro-security policies go together. Faster growth makes it easier to pay for things like Social Security and a stronger safety net. Conversely, more fairness and better economic security makes it easier for Americans to accept the uncertainty and tumult of technology-led growth.

A new political coalition in favor of exuberant growth will cut across traditional party lines, encompassing the groups that benefited from the 1990s: investors, the educated class, and the less educated workers. It will push hard for pro-growth policies such as increased support for R&D, education, and a risk-taking financial system. And it will push equally hard for pro-security policies, such as transparency, income insurance, and an improved safety net. This is the best way that the U.S. can succeed.

WHY A COALITION FOR GROWTH IS NECESSARY

If there's any lesson that should be taken away from this book, it's that exuberant growth is a tough sell. Both new technology and financial markets are vulnerable to pressure from enemies of growth and from existing companies. The only way that technology-driven growth can be sustained is if a broad coalition can be convinced that it is in their interests.

That's not necessarily easy. There's no obvious constituency for higher levels of spending on R&D and increased funding for graduate education in science and engineering. The payoff for basic research, for example, lies years away.

Moreover, every new technology brings up unprecedented issues of safety, ethics, and financing, as well as conflicts with existing businesses. All of these have to be mediated by government bureaucrats and politicians, who are susceptible to public and private pressure and lobbying. Depending on their actions, the adoption of new technologies can either be slowed down or expedited.

That's been true since the early days of the railroads in the 1800s. Originally there was tremendous opposition to the construction of railroads by operators of canals and stage lines, by farmers who feared a decline in the market for horses and hay, by tavernkeepers who saw a falloff in business from stage and wagon travel, and by journalists who scorned new railroads. One newspaper criticized a railroad line from Boston to Albany as

> a project which everyone knows who knows the simplest rule of arithmetic to be impracticable, but at an expense little less than the market value of the whole territory of Massachusetts; and which, if practicable, every person of common sense knows would be as useless as a railroad from Boston to the moon.

State legislators defended the rights of the canals against the steel-railed interlopers. The 1848 railroad incorporation act in New York required railroads to pay tolls to any canals within 30 miles.

But then the attitude of the public and the government flipped around as the value of the new technology became clear. Many states funded the construction of railroads within their boundaries, with Virginia, for example, giving a total of $21 million in the years before the Civil War. From 1862 onward, the federal government gave away large land grants to western railroads to help fund their construction, accounting for perhaps 7 percent of the continental U.S.

Today, the hodgepodge of regulation and deregulation in telecom has slowed down the rollout of broadband. The question is whether there is popular support for a policy that would encourage the extension of broadband service to more homes, either by subsidies or by tax incentives.

More generally, the political climate also plays a key role in the fate of financial markets, which are so essential to U.S. growth prospects. Financial markets are particularly vulnerable to government interference, since they are already regulated closely. In their book, *Saving Capitalism from the Capitalists,* Raghuram Rajan and Luigi Zingales discuss what they call the "Great Reversal"–the shift away from free financial markets after the Great Depression:

> Perhaps the least understood of markets, the most unfairly
> criticized, and the one most critical to making a country
> competitive is the financial market. It is also the market that
> is most sensitive to the political winds.

Today, the distrust of the financial system is playing out on several fronts, including the intense pressure to roll back or limit stock options. If that happens, it will hurt a key competitive edge of the U.S.

BUILDING A COALITION

For all of these reasons, sustainable exuberant growth will not happen without a solid base of support. The likeliest members of this coalition are the groups who prospered in the 1990s, and who are likely to do well in another round of exuberant growth. Unfortunately, those are the same people who are exposed to the unpredictability of technology-driven growth.

One group that logically should favor exuberant growth is investors in the stock market. When signs of a new technological breakthrough begin to appear, they are immediately translated into soaring prices for the stocks of the companies that are the presumed leaders. Of course, that leaves those same investors vulnerable if the new technology falls short and sends the stock crashing to earth, as happened during the tech and telecom bust.

The second group that should be friendly toward exuberant growth is the members of the educated class. As we will see in more detail in the next chapter, workers with a college degree seem to prosper in periods of rapid technological change, because they have the higher-level skills necessary to cope with and improve cutting-edge innovations. However, because educated workers are at the top of the heap already, they have more worries because they have a lot farther to fall.

The final group that did well in the 1990s was workers toward the bottom of the pay scale. For example, real (inflation-adjusted) wages for equipment cleaners, helpers, and nonfarm laborers—generally employed at low-skill, low-paying jobs—rose by 9 percent between 1993 and 2003, after dropping by 6 percent between 1983 and 1993. (These figures are all calculated based on data from the Bureau of Labor Statistics.) Real wages for retail workers, another poorly paid group, rose by 7 percent between 1993 and 2003, after dropping by 2 percent between 1983 and 1993.

Low-paid workers, such as these folks, do much better in periods of rapid productivity growth. However, they are more concerned with safety and security than anyone else, because they don't have the financial resources to cope well with the volatility in the economy.

These groups cut across the traditional political dividing line, of Democrats and Republicans. In that sense, this period bears certain similarities to the Progressive era of the late 1800s and early 1900s. That was a period of rapid technological change and rapid productivity growth, and like today, punctuated by scandals and financial crises.

Moreover, that era was also graced by antitechnology "enemies of growth," in the form of the Populist movement. For the Populists—based primarily in the Midwest and the South—the main objective was to protect farmers from falling prices and from being taken advantage of by the rapidly growing industrial sector. The core platform of populism included public ownership of the economy's leading-edge industries: telegraph, telephones, and especially the railroads, which were accused of overcharging farmers for transporting their crops.

According to one economic historian:

> The utopia conjured up in the populist imagination was oriented to the past rather than to the future. Populism was a movement bent upon restoring the harassed farmer to a former happier estate largely superseded by an industrial order in which a predatory minority enriched itself from the labor of the masses.

The Populist movement eventually faltered. Nevertheless, government policies during the Progressive era included support for both pro-growth and pro-security policies, under both Republican and Democratic presidents. Generally the government was open to both free trade and new technologies, such as electricity, automobiles, and radio. At the same time, the list of reform legislation included the Sherman Antitrust Act of 1890, which was passed under President Benjamin Harrison, a Republican, and used by Theodore Roosevelt, another Republican, to go after Standard Oil. Other consumer and worker protection actions included the creation of the Federal Trade Commission in 1914, the Pure Food and Drug Act of 1906, child labor laws, and state regulation of railroads and public utilities.

Of course, we won't see the passage of that many new regulations ever again. But the combination of pro-growth and pro-security policies is a good model for today.

PRO-SECURITY AND FAIRNESS

Finding the right combination of pro-security policies is more difficult, because it's necessary to address the concerns of all three groups in the potential coalition for exuberant growth. What's needed is a blend of policies.

THE PRINCIPLE OF TRANSPARENCY

Even now—years after the Enron and WorldCom scandals broke—we have limited information about what most big American companies are really doing. Financial disclosure is incomplete and potentially misleading.

Moreover, the very lack of information creates a distrust and unease that slows down the introduction and acceptance of new technologies. All of the potential breakthroughs listed in the previous chapter have to overcome technical, economic, and safety barriers. The problem is that the acceptance barrier becomes even higher if ordinary people feel that they cannot believe the companies.

And it's not just financial information. Transparency is essential for the introduction and acceptance of new technologies. The more that Americans feel something is being hidden from them, the less likely they are to trust the scientists and companies who say that everything is okay. Every lie or omission—no matter how well intended—is one step toward confirming the fear that something worse is lurking. Innovation must be done in the sunlight in order to maintain political support.

In the exuberant economy, the best alternative to direct regulation is the principle of *transparency*. That means being willing to open up the inner workings of a corporation or an agency of the government—to provide essential information that would otherwise not be available.

Better information helps Americans—in their various roles as investors, workers, and voters—make better decisions about what risks to take. In a slow-moving cautious economy, lack of information is an inconvenience but not an overwhelming problem. Corporations don't move very quickly, there are relatively few new technologies, and those are introduced slowly and incrementally. But in a fast-paced exuberant economy, the lack of information means that you are flying blind.

Access to information also provides a useful check on bad decision by managers, either attempts to line their own pockets or simply mistakes. Markets work better when the participants have more information, and are better able to monitor the behavior and performance of managers.

Finally, transparency is absolutely essential for fairness. In retrospect, one of the biggest complaints about the 1990s is that too many people got ahead by cheating. From the Nasdaq collapse to the mutual funds scandal, the common thread is concealment and use of inside information—for example, the exact stocks held in a mutual fund. Widespread distribution of information levels the playing field, and gives even the poor a better chance of taking advantage of new opportunities.

Over the last several years, regulators have made an effort to increase the amount of information available to investors. For example, in December 1999 the Securities and Exchange Commission proposed what it called Regulation FD (for "fair disclosure"). The regulation was put into effect in October 2000, with the requirement that any "material nonpublic information" disclosed to investors or analysts had to be released publicly as well.

In the aftermath of the latest corporate scandals, there has been a series of regulatory rulings and new laws attempting to provide more information about what goes on behind closed corporate doors. The Sarbanes-Oxley legislation, passed in 2002, requires companies to rapidly report "material events" such as the loss of a major customer. Off-balance-sheet transactions, such as the ones that got Enron into trouble, will in general have to be disclosed. And insiders have to report their trades in company stock within a couple of days of the transaction.

But let's be honest. The new regulations are more like boring a little peephole into the inner corporate sanctum than opening a door or even a window. Even after Sarbanes-Oxley went into full effect, corporate financial reports still omit a truckload of information that would help current shareholders and potential investors, as well as workers, judge the efficiency and productivity of the company.

For example, better reporting on costs—particularly wage and benefit costs—would be very helpful to investors trying to assess the efficiency of a company. Hard as it may be to believe, most corporations don't break down their wage and benefit costs separately on their financial reports. Instead they generally combine them with other costs of production.

It also makes sense for companies to provide a more detailed breakdown of the distribution of revenue and employees, by line of business and country. Right now most companies offer the minimum amount of information about where sales are coming from. Workforce costs are reported on a companywide basis, without any breakdown by country at all. That makes it very hard for investors to assess trends in outsourcing.

And finally, one of the most important–and most difficult– steps on the road to transparency is to open up tax returns to the public. While that sounds like a dramatic step, there's historical precedent. When the corporate income tax–then called the "corporation excise tax"–was introduced in 1909, tax returns were public. The need for openness and more information was one of the reasons why the corporate tax was originally passed.

Congress took the teeth out of the disclosure within a few years, as companies complained it would disclose important information to their competitors, and disadvantage small companies relative to big ones. Still, something similar now could be very effective as a way of getting more disclosure.

INCOME INSURANCE

One of the big sources of stress in the pulsating market is the higher levels of variability in income from year to year. All sorts of events can befall people, either voluntarily or involuntarily. New technology can affect your work, for better or for worse. The economy can go through a boom-and-bust cycle. You can join a start-up and accept a pay cut, and it can either fail or go spectacularly public and make you a ton of money.

This is not just an economic issue—it's an emotional issue as well. Even if a college-educated worker is doing well, there's the fear something could happen tomorrow. That argues for initiating some form of *income insurance*. It would help soothe the fears, and make educated workers more comfortable with exuberant growth.

In part, this problem has been ameliorated by the development of the consumer credit market. It's far easier than ever before to cover up a temporary loss of income with credit cards, home equity, or other borrowing.

But there's also a simple way to provide income insurance through the tax code, if we are willing to tinker just a bit. That's by allowing *income averaging,* and giving taxpayers the option of paying taxes as if their income was averaged over three years.

Adding an income averaging provision to the tax code would have the effect of allowing a laid-off worker to collect a sizable tax refund. The exact amount would differ depending on income and the length of time out of work, but it could be on the order of 30–40 percent of the taxes paid. That's not insignificant.

How does this work? The current tax system actually penalizes people whose income changes sharply from one year to the next. Because the tax system is progressive, higher incomes get taxed at a higher rate. That means a person who has a high income one year and a low income the next will typically pay a higher total tax than someone who has the same total income, but spread out over two or three years.

As a result, the tax system penalizes both job-losers and risk-takers. People who have more variable income—because they own their own businesses, or because they are freelancers—can expect to pay higher taxes on average than non-risk-takers.

For example, a married couple who makes $60,000 a year in taxable income (after deductions and exemptions) for two years pays $8,620 a year in federal income taxes, or $17,240 total. (These simple examples are based on the revised 2003 tax rate schedules, ignoring complicating factors such as the phaseout of deductions.)

Now consider another married couple who make $120,000 in taxable income in one year and nothing the next year, either because they have variable income or because the working spouse has lost his or her job. This second couple has to send the IRS $23,780 in income taxes the first year, and nothing the second.

If we compare the two situations, we see that the two couples earn the same amount, $120,000, totaled over two years. But the second couple pays almost 40 percent more in taxes!

That's simply not fair. Two households who have the exact same amount of income over two years should not have to pay substantially different taxes—especially when it's the unemployed couple, or the one with the riskier job, who is paying more.

There's a simple way to remove this penalty: Allow taxpayers to average their income over three years. That would go a long way toward cushioning the blow of being laid off, as well as making it easier for people to take risks.

For example, suppose that a worker gets laid off from a job at which he or she is earning $180,000 annually in taxable income. Then if he or she is out of work for one year, and files for income averaging, the size of the refund will equal roughly $10,000. That's not an enormous sum, but it's enough to pay the grocery bills for many American families (according to the Bureau of Labor Statistics, the average household spends about $5,000 per year on food; for households in the top 20 percent of the income distribution, that number jumps to roughly $9,000 per year on food).

Nor is income averaging foreign to the tax code. In fact, there's plenty of precedent. Until it was repealed by the tax reform of 1986, Americans who saw their income take a big jump could average it. And the current tax code has included income averaging for farmers since the Taxpayer Relief Act of 1997. That law allowed farmers to average their income over three years, including years with losses.

IMPROVING THE SAFETY NET

The third piece of the puzzle is a better safety net. In particular, that means both improving unemployment insurance and providing some form of health insurance for the unemployed. The details of such plans have been explored at excruciating length over the last decade and are not necessary here. However, no matter what approach was taken, better unemployment and health coverage would go a long way toward ameliorating the pain and distress of technological change and globalization. Moreover, it's much more appealing to leave an employer and start a new business if you know that you won't lose your health insurance in the process.

Certainly any proposal to boost the safety net will run into intense headwinds, since it would represent a break in a 20-year trend toward less protection by government. The "safety net" has been under attack since the days of Ronald Reagan, at a time when slow growth made it very difficult to pay for extensive social programs. "I believe it is clear our Federal Government is overgrown and overweight," said Reagan in his July 17, 1980, speech accepting the nomination. "It is time our Government should go on a diet."

Since then, opponents of the safety net have argued that such programs are simply too expensive, pointing out that Social Security and Medicare alone absorb a big chunk of GDP. They say that such programs are not fair, redistributing income from honest taxpayers to ne'er-do-wells. Finally, with some justification opponents argue that the existence of a safety net makes recipients more dependent on government aid, and less able to fend for themselves. It reduces the incentives to get the skills needed to actually find a good job. As the saying goes: "Give a man a fish and it'll feed him for a day; teach him how to fish and it'll feed him for a lifetime."

In a cautious economy, these three arguments against the safety net—expense, fairness, incentives—are persuasive. But in an exuberant economy, the objections to expanding the safety net have far less weight. Consider expense first. Providing protection is certainly costly, but the burden is much easier to bear when growth is faster. The original Reagan attacks against the safety net came in the second half of the 1970s, when the economy was mired in a low-innovation, slow-growth quagmire. When times are tough, it's harder to find compassion for others. But when the economy is expanding rapidly, it's easier to divert some to the needy.

What about fairness? A cautious economy has less mobility, so that social programs always seem to be benefiting the same groups. By contrast, in an exuberant economy, technological change can affect anyone's job, and insecurity is always right around the corner. That's true even in apparently protected areas such as health care, which could be greatly affected by advances in biotech. For example, it's possible that new drugs could require fewer but more highly trained personnel, which would greatly transform the nursing workforce.

Finally, an improved safety net is much less harmful to worker incentives in an exuberant economy than in a cautious economy. When growth is slow, the major incentives motivating workers are negative ones: the threat of unemployment and poverty. Thus, anything that reduces those threats has the potential to weaken work incentives.

By contrast, in an exuberant economy, the positive incentives can be stronger. With strong growth and good wage increases, workers have a reason to care about their performance, even without the threat of unemployment. More important, employers can use positive incentives such as stock options to motivate employees. In an exuberant economy, the possibility of getting rich makes it less likely that the presence or absence of a safety net will affect work effort.

PROSPECTS FOR AN EXUBERANT GROWTH COALITION

Putting together an exuberant growth coalition won't be easy. For one thing, the core groups of both parties—the religious conservatives and deficit hawks on the Republican side, and unions and liberals on the Democratic side—are uncomfortable with rapid technological change.

And the individual pro-security and fairness proposals will generate opposition as well. Big business opposes transparency. Anything that smacks of income insurance will upset free market conservatives, while the big tax breaks provided by income averaging will raise the ire of both deficit hawks and liberals who have been fighting the Bush tax cuts. And an improved safety net will bring all sorts of opponents out of the woodwork, just as every attempt to reform health insurance does.

What's needed is political leadership able to make the connection that better economic security actually improves the chances of getting stronger economic growth. That's not a link that the Clinton administration was willing or able to make, and it's not something that the Bush administration has tried to do either.

In the end, running on a platform of security *and* technology-led growth may be the best way to assemble the sort of sustainable political base that wins elections—and keeps the country growing.

CHAPTER 10

Will the Education Bubble Burst?

A failure to form a workable coalition for exuberant growth will have serious consequences. In particular, the group most at risk is the educated class. They have prospered because the rapid introduction of new technology puts a premium on hiring workers who are adaptable, creative, and able to handle change.

But if the U.S. is entering an era of cautious technological consolidation—building on old advances rather than creating new ones—employers are likely to decide that having an educated and creative workforce is less important than having an inexpensive one. In that case, the premium for having a college education will start to shrink significantly for the first time in 20 years.

What's worse, a technological slowdown, if it happens, will come at a particularly vulnerable time for the U.S. educated class. The number of new college grads is much higher than anyone expected just a few years ago, creating a potential oversupply of college-educated workers. As of 2002, almost 27 percent of Americans had completed college, up sharply from 23 percent in 1995. At the same time, countries such as India and China have dramatically increased spending on higher education, producing a lot more college grads and creating a potent workforce of educated competitors.

The danger is that it will start feeling like the 1970s again—a period when a lack of innovation was accompanied by a sharp and sudden drop in incomes for educated workers. Without another technological revolution, the educated class will be stuck—with less demand for their special talents, and mounting competition at home and abroad. The value of human capital would come crashing down—the 20-year education boom could turn out to have been an education bubble, which would pop with catastrophic consequences.

If the education boom does come to an abrupt end, that will almost certainly be the compelling economic and political fact of the next few years. Dealing with the collapse of the education bubble will affect every part of the economy and the national psyche—including a breakdown in the coalition for exuberant growth.

THE LAST EDUCATION BUST: THE 1970S

We're used to an economy that favors the educated. But to find a time when things were different, just look back to the 1970s. From 1975 to 1981, the average earnings for college graduates fell by 9 percent, adjusted for inflation, according to figures from the Census Bureau. Real earnings for holders of advanced degrees fell even more sharply, by 11 percent.

That was an era when there were stories of Ph.D.s driving

taxicabs, and a general sense of "underemployment" among the highly educated. In a 1977 survey, 44 percent of young college graduates said that they were underemployed in their current positions. "The economic rewards to a college education are markedly lower than has historically been the case," wrote Harvard economist Richard Freeman in his 1976 book, *The Overeducated American.* "Education has become, like investments in other mature industries or activities, a marginal rather than highly profitable endeavor."

The joke was that plumbers would do better than doctors. A proud father was showing a fellow worker a picture of his five grown sons. His friend asked what they did for a living. The father said the older two are doctors and the youngest two are lawyers. The friend asked about the middle son, and the father said, "Oh, he's a plumber. Someone had to pay for all the others' educations."

Why did wages for educated workers lag in the 1970s? In part, it was because the graduating classes of colleges were swollen by kids who had gone to college in the late 1960s to avoid the draft. That created a temporary oversupply of college graduates.

Perhaps more important, the second half of the 1970s was an era of slow or no technological change. That took away one of the main advantages of being educated, the ability to adapt to new ways of doing things. After all, who needs expensive employees with college degrees when nothing is changing very fast?

In 1976, Jerome Wiesner, then president of MIT, wrote about the "slowing down of the innovative process." A couple of years later, *BusinessWeek* ran a cover story titled "Vanishing Innovation," which argued that "a hostile climate for new ideas and products is threatening the technological superiority of the U.S."

The lack of technological progress showed up in the official economic data as well. From 1973 to 1983, the government's statistics of productivity showed very little contribution from technological change. And patents—a useful measure of new technologies—peaked at 78,000 in 1971 and slid downward in the 1970s and early 1980s, hitting less than 57,000 in 1983.

Meanwhile, there were no new technologies that made a major dent in the marketplace in the late 1970s. The personal computer revolution was just in its very earliest stages. Apple didn't sell its first computer with a disk drive—a prerequisite for making it something more than a plaything for hobbyists—until the middle of 1978. The first IBM PC, of course, didn't come out until 1981.

THE EDUCATION BOOM

Roughly around the same time that IBM released its first PC, the job market for educated workers turned up, and hasn't stopped since. For the last 20 years, educated Americans have lived a privileged existence. Real wages for college-educated workers have risen most years, and their unemployment rate has stayed low, even during recessions.

The more education a worker had, the better. From 1980 to 2000, real earnings for bachelor's degree holders went up by 31 percent. People with advanced degrees such as doctors, lawyers, and professors saw their earnings go up by 46 percent. (That's based on data from the Census Bureau.) By comparison, earnings for high school graduates, adjusted for inflation, went up by only 9 percent over the same stretch.

Getting a college degree lowered the odds of being unemployed as well. From 1992 to 2002, the average unemployment rate for college-educated workers was a stunningly low 2.4 percent. That was roughly half the average rate of 4.8 percent for workers with a high school degree and no college. Moreover, much of that

2.4 percent represented "frictional" unemployment–people simply taking off some time between jobs, rather than true unemployment.

That meant educated workers were able to go about their lives without worrying very much about risk. They've been able to spend and take on big mortgage debts without fear that they will be out of work for an extended period. College graduates have been able to join start-ups, invest in the stock market, try out new technologies, support deregulation and globalization, and generally take big risks both in their personal life and work life, without bearing the consequences.

The sharp rise in the stock market, which started in 1982, primarily benefited educated Americans, who were more likely to own stocks. Similarly, because college graduates had home-ownership rates around 70 percent–greater than the rest of the the population–they were the biggest beneficiaries of the appreciation in housing prices over the last two decades.

Surprisingly, even the bust of 2000, 2001, and 2002 didn't do much to erode the advantage of educated workers in the labor market. True, plenty of people had real complaints about losing money in the stock market. And layoffs–especially at the companies at the epicenter of the tech bust–hurt a lot of educated Americans. Employment in the computer systems design industry fell by 16 percent from its peak in early 2001 to the fall of 2003.

But taken as a whole, most of the educated class continued to prosper right through the downturn and into the recovery. Unemployment for college-educated workers never rose above 3.2 percent, despite all the media attention to white-collar jobs being moved overseas. That's lower than the peak of college-educated unemployment in the early 1990s.

All the other statistics from the Bureau of Labor Statistics

(BLS) also painted a picture of an educated workforce that, if not buoyant, was at least holding its own. Between November 2000 and November 2003, the number of employed college grads aged 25 and over rose by about 3 million, or 9 percent. Meanwhile, employment of Americans with less than a college education fell by 500,000 over that same stretch.

Similarly, people in high-end jobs did much better in terms of wages even during the bust years. According to the official numbers from the BLS, wages and salaries for managers and executives rose by 6 percent from 2000 to 2003, adjusted for inflation. By comparison, real wages and salaries for production and nonsupervisory workers went up by only 3 percent over that three-year period.

TECHNOLOGY AND EDUCATION

Surprisingly, even during the bust years, the wage gap between college-educated workers and the rest of the population has continued to widen. In a relative sense, the educated class has become even more expensive. The share of college grads in the workforce has grown until they now comprise 33 percent of employed adults and almost half of all wage costs, making them a target for any company that wants to cut costs. In a word, they are vulnerable.

Still, college-educated workers have one big advantage: They are better able to cope with a rapid pace of change. They are more able to make adjustments on the fly, imagine and develop new products and strategies. "One important part of the value of a college education is that it better prepares the student for a lifetime of learning and change," writes Leonard Nakamura, an economist at the Federal Reserve Bank of Philadelphia. "Indeed, the ideal of the liberal college education is one of preparing a broad base for continuing learning."

For example, the Internet Revolution, in its early years, was based on a do-it-yourself mentality. People curious and resourceful enough to surf the Net in the early 1990s had to learn arcane terms such as "telnet," "gopher," "WAIS," and "ftp." They had to have some measure of literacy and logical thinking, and the ability to figure out complicated puzzles—because that's what the Internet was in its early years. Even after the browser was introduced, the Internet was a mystery that required some degree of intelligence to work with.

Thus, as information technology has pushed into the workplace over the past decade, it's put a premium on people who are quickly able to learn new skills, and figure out new ways to use the technology. In fact, an entire industry of information technology consultants has grown up around the need to provide companies with the help that they need. The number of people working in consulting firms has doubled since the early 1990s, and the number of people working in firms doing computer systems design has tripled over the same stretch (even after the bust).

THE PERILS OF SLOW INNOVATION

But what if the rate of change slows? What happens after most businesses have been computerized, networked, Web-enabled? If there are fewer new must-have technologies, then we slip back to the 1970s again. The ability to cope with change becomes less valuable, and businesses have an incentive to reduce their use of expensive educated labor. The forces of gravity will begin to reassert themselves, and it will become far harder to justify paying a college grad with a B.A. 60 percent more than someone with an associate's degree who can do the same job. In a world of slow innovation, it will become apparent very quickly that the pay for educated workers is way out of line with fundamentals–and the whole thing will come crashing to the ground.

It is precisely the routinization of technology that poses a deep and hidden danger for the educated class. As a task becomes more routine, it is more amenable to being computerized, so that it requires a lower level of skill and education. In a 2003 paper, economists David Autor, Frank Levy, and Richard Murnane observe:

> Computer capital substitutes for workers in carrying out a limited and well-defined set of cognitive and manual activities, those that can be accomplished by following explicit rules (what we term "routine tasks").

The set of routine tasks expands over time. Building even a simple Web site was difficult in the early days of the Internet, but over time it became as easy as clicking on a button in a program. More broadly, the task of operating a personal computer became something routine, that almost anyone could do.

To put it a different way, if the economy stops pushing its way into new technological territory, educated workers are in danger of seeing their jobs "deskilled." That term, first popularized in the 1970s, means that the education and judgment content of a job is reduced so that it can be done by less-skilled, lower-paid workers, either in the U.S. or overseas.

In such a world, fears of being "deskilled" will pervade the entire educated class. Programmers will worry about being replaced by cheaper labor in India and the Philippines. College professors will worry about being replaced by distance education. Librarians will see themselves becoming nothing but glorified nursemaids for Internet terminals. The educated class will no longer feel immune from the trials and tribulations of the economy.

Certainly history offers no guarantees for educated workers–

quite the opposite. There have been plenty of times in the past when skilled workers were undermined by new inventions and techniques–a technological coup d'état, as it were. "The idea that technological advances favor more skilled workers is a twentieth century phenomenon," writes Daron Acemoglu, an MIT economist.

Many innovations of the 19th century and early 20th century–including factory mass production–were aimed squarely at replacing skilled workers with machines and unskilled workers. The privileged position of skilled artisans and craftsmen was gradually eroded by technology. Almost anything that could be produced by hand–expensively–could be made–cheaply–in a factory. That's not a precedent that should be reassuring to educated workers today.

FEELING THE DOWNDRAFT

For the last 20 years, a college degree has been the rarest of anomalies–a low-risk, high-return asset. College grads have enjoyed low-risk work lives, because low unemployment rates mean that they are rarely out of work. And with their wages rising much faster than inflation, returns have been high as well.

However, as a general rule, high-return, low-risk investments are ephemeral. It is rare for them to last, because such an attractive investment would draw a flood of new money. It would be like the stock market always going up, without any risk of a downturn–and as we have seen over the last few years, that situation can't last forever.

In fact, the supply of college-educated labor has been rising, both at home and globally. For one thing, over the last couple of years there has been an increase in college enrollments in the U.S., driven by a combination of the carrot and the stick. The carrot was the steadily increasing wage premium for college graduates, making it more attractive to have a degree. The stick was the weakness of the labor market since the bust, which makes being in school a better option than looking for a job. For example, the enrollment at Ohio State University rose from 55,737 in the autumn quarter of 2001 to 58,254 in the autumn quarter of 2003. Similarly, the full-time enrollment at the campuses of the University of California rose from 183,355 in fall 2000 to 201,297 in fall 2002, a 10 percent increase.

All told, the latest numbers from the BLS show that the number of college graduates in the labor force rose by an astonishing 5.7 percent from November 2002 to November 2003, or 2.2 million additional college-educated workers. That's compared with a 3.2 percent annual increase from 1992 to 2002.

And then there's the foreign education boom. Ever since the 1970s, blue-collar workers in the U.S. have kept one nervous eye on their counterparts in other countries. For factory workers, foreign competition has been part of their lives for decades—and not a particularly pleasant part. Industry after industry has simply vanished from the U.S., to reappear in China, in Mexico, and a dozen other countries.

For U.S. college grads it has been a different story. Until recently, globalization was only a positive for the educated class. People who received college diplomas in the 1960s, 1970s, or even 1980s had an unfair advantage that they didn't even realize at the time. They grew up in a world in which there was very little competition from overseas for their type of cerebral, persuasive, or organizational activities. Compared with the guy who worked at the widget factory down the street and worried about his job leaving the country, they were sitting pretty.

The reason was very simple: The other major economies simply did not have the college-trained population to compete with American college grads. Take the generation now aged 45–54, for example, who roughly correspond to people who got their college degrees 25–35 years ago. In the U.S., 30 percent of people in that age group have a college education. In Japan and Germany, the percentage of college-educated people in that age group was only about 15. In France, the percentage of college graduates was only about 10. That was no way to run a modern economy.

As noted in Chapter 6, that's changed, not just in the advanced countries but in China and India as well. Today, the surge in college enrollment overseas is creating an enormous overhang of low-cost college graduates, which can potentially replace the much more expensive U.S. graduates.

A VICIOUS CIRCLE

At the start of the 1980s, people with any sort of a college education, even the briefest exposure to college, were a distinct minority. Now they are the dominant economic and political force in the country. Almost half of all wage income goes to households headed by someone with a college education. More than 60 percent of voters in 2000 had at least some college.

That dominance of the educated class was good for exuberant growth in the 1980s and 1990s. It was a virtuous circle: College-educated workers benefited from technology and globalization, without much risk. They therefore were willing, by and large, to accept and even encourage technological change and free trade.

But if technological change slows, unemployment will rise and wages will fall. It will become harder to persuade those with power and influence that innovation and change is in their interest. The downside from uncertainty and turmoil will seem much more real than any possible gains from new technology.

Paradoxically, a slowdown in innovation could be the spur for a neo-Luddite movement. Recall that the Luddites—the best-known objectors to technology—were an early-19th-century group of workers, based mainly in Nottinghamshire (the mythical home of Robin Hood). Over the course of five years, 1811 to 1816, they conducted a campaign against the installation of new knitting frames. They broke machines and threatened the owners of the businesses that used them.

The Luddites did not succeed. Even though their name still resonates today, they were unable to stop or even slow down the Industrial Revolution. Similarly, factory workers today did not have enough political clout to slow down globalization.

However, if the educated elite start feeling betrayed by technology and globalization, the results might be different. The educated and sophisticated are far better placed to slow down new technologies than their less-educated brethren.

It will become a vicious circle, as slowing innovation creates turmoil and uncertainty, which only erodes the support for technological change and exuberant growth. It will be harder to tempt people to join start-ups, harder to take chances on the stock market, harder to take risks in general. The popping of the education bubble will mire the U.S. in cautious growth.

CHAPTER 11

The Worst-Case Scenario

As this book is written, the recovery is well under way, with growth topping 8 percent in the third quarter of 2003, and solid gains seemingly in place for the fourth quarter. With this in mind, even if technological change slows, how bad could things get?

The answer is pretty bad—and these negative possibilities may have powerful and distressing consequences for the U.S. economy, for national security, and for the rest of the world.

FALSE MOMENTUM

As we learned in middle school, Newton's First Law states that a body in motion will tend to stay in motion. This is the concept of "momentum." It applies to all manner of physical objects, from baseballs, to shopping carts, to freight trains. A baseball thrown by a child will leave his or her hand, and keep flying until it breaks a window. A train heading down the tracks at 60 miles per hour will tend to continue to travel at that speed unless the engineer puts on the brakes. Even then, it may take a mile or more for the train to stop—bad news if you are in a car stalled on the tracks.

Economists and journalists like to carry over the physical analogy to the economic world, and use the world "momentum" to talk about the economy. For example, in early 2002, the Conference Board—a New York–based management group—reported that the economy was "gathering momentum." But then by late 2002, the president of the Federal Reserve Bank of Philadelphia worried in a speech that the economy appeared "to have lost momentum."

This analogy to the physical world gives the sense that the economy slows down or speeds up smoothly, just like a train or a supertanker would. It encourages the conclusion that the economy is unlikely to make abrupt starts or stops, or suddenly change direction dramatically. And it makes the U.S. economy, with 145 million workers and $30 billion in output per *day*, seem as steady and hard to turn in its course as a supertanker.

In fact, most economic forecasting models—including the one used by the Federal Reserve—have "momentum" built into them. When you dig down deep into the inner workings of the forecasting models—deep enough to get raw bits and bytes under your fingernails—the models are effectively built on an assumption about what the sustainable growth rate of the economy is today.

Such reasoning leads to a reassuring conclusion: That slow growth of 2001, 2002, and early 2003 is really just a temporary response to some bad shocks—the end of the investment bubble, the terrorist attacks, the Iraq war. And once the recovery really gets going, it will be self-sustaining.

A SHARP TURN?

But the physical analogy is highly misleading. Economies do not have inertia or momentum. The historical record indicates that one minute they can be zooming along at top speed, with seemingly no problem, and the next minute they are heading deep into a slump.

And not just a short, mild slump, either. Countries can switch from being fast-growth paragons to slow-growth drudges in a blink of an eye. The most recent example of this Jekyll and Hyde act, of course, is Japan, which followed up 30 years of rapid growth, ending in 1989, with 10 years of very little or no growth at all. Germany and Switzerland experienced the same problem.

These are not isolated cases. "Relatively few countries have done consistently well, and averaging over long periods tends to obscure the episodic nature of growth," concluded one 1999 survey of the growth literature. "Frequently countries have done well for short periods, only for growth to collapse later on." Countries such as Brazil, Mexico, and Chile had rapid growth of living standards in the 1970s, followed by weak or slow growth in the 1980s.

What does this have to do with the worst-case scenario? The implication is simple: Clear your mind of the assumption that the rapid productivity growth of the recent period will necessarily carry over to the coming years. Alan Greenspan said it well himself in an October 2002 speech:

> History does raise some warning flags concerning the length of time that productivity growth continues elevated. Gains in productivity remained quite rapid for years after the innovations that followed the surge of inventions a century ago. But in other episodes, the period of elevated growth of productivity was shorter. Regrettably, examples are too few to generalize.

In other words, it's reassuring to assume that productivity gains will necessarily continue—but nothing in history gives us that surety.

WHEN THINGS GO BAD

Let's consider the worst-case scenario, in which technological change slows. As described in the last chapter, the education bubble would pop, and political support for exuberant growth would evaporate. The economy would shift, decisively, to cautious growth and risk-taking would become much less common.

If we take that path, the next 10 years would look more like the 1970s, economically, than like the 1990s. Growth would be driven by the slow and steady accumulation of capital, rather than by innovation, as it was during the boom years. The winners would be the big companies with capital and market power, rather than the small nimble start-ups.

Let's put that into numbers. In the decade from 1993 to 2003, output per worker rose at a 2.8 percent annual rate. Over the previous 20 years, it rose at a 1.4 percent annual rate. In the worst case, productivity growth would shift down to an even lower number, 1 percent annually.

Such a slowdown sounds innocuous. After all, increasing output per worker by 2.8 percent in a year doesn't seem to be that much different from increasing it by 1 percent. To put it into mundane terms, it would be like investing $10 and getting back a return of 10 cents rather than 28 cents. That hardly seems like much of a bother at all.

But just as pennies add up over time, so do the differences in productivity. Such a downshift in productivity growth, if it persists, is one of the most dangerous things that can happen to an economy. Workers and companies get used to rapid productivity growth—and when it stops, it's like running into a brick wall.

THE POSSIBLE GROWTH CRISIS

Viewed from the perspective of the enemies of growth, such a downshift to cautious growth doesn't sound so appalling. The reality, though, is that an unexpected shift to cautious growth creates a "growth crisis," with widespread ramifications. The previous chapter described one of the main effects, the slowdown in the demand for educated workers. But in fact everything slows down—productivity growth slows, wage growth slows, home price appreciation (adjusted for inflation) slows, and the stock market weakens as profit growth slows.

Historically, such growth crises—marked by big and unexpected downward shifts in growth rates—are more common than we realize. Every major industrialized country has experienced a major growth crisis sometime in the last 30 years, with the latest being Germany and Japan in the 1990s. For both of these countries, the growth crisis started at the beginning of the 1990s. The last U.S. growth crisis started in the middle of the 1970s.

Let's clearly distinguish a growth crisis from a recession. A recession is a temporary contraction in output and employment, with emphasis on the word "temporary" without any change in the long-term rate of growth. It's like bending to tie your shoelace—for the moment your head is lower than it usually is, but once you stand up you return to your original height. In the same way, once the economy recovers from a recession, it returns back to its original growth path.

As a result, recessions bring a mixture of optimism and pessimism about the future, because people always have hope that things will get better when the recovery comes. By contrast, when a growth crisis hits, it produces a kind of despondency. What Keynes called animal spirits depart, and people worry more about protecting what they have, rather than taking risks for the future.

Once the growth crisis strikes, trouble piles up. The problem is that during the exuberant period, people and companies take on debt and make investments under the assumption that the economy will continue to grow at a rapid pace. That shows up very clearly in the housing market, where home buyers are willing to pay higher prices because they expect the value of their homes to appreciate. Moreover, the expectation that salaries will continue to rise justifies the decision to buy a home, even at a high price.

Similarly, when companies expect faster growth in the future, it's completely obvious that they will be more willing to borrow and to add new capacity now. But then when the growth crisis hits and growth suddenly slows, all of a sudden that capacity and that debt becomes much harder to service. That's what happened to Japan in the 1990s. Banks had made loans under the expectation that the economy would keep growing at a rapid rate. When it didn't, loan losses were far greater than anyone expected.

The full impact of a growth crisis does not usually hit until well after the recession is over. During the initial stages of recovery, growth is almost always strong, as the depressed parts of the economy bounce back. For that reason, the beginning of a growth crisis is often hard to identify at the time. In retrospect, the 1974–75 recession marked the onset of the last U.S. growth crisis. Nevertheless, the recovery was very strong, with growth averaging more than 5 percent annually in the three years that followed the recession. The economic data at the time gave no hard evidence of a deterioration of the economy, though several years later, after several revisions and updates, the productivity slowdown was clear.

Under the surface, what was happening was that Americans

were working more and more, but feeling worse and worse. In July 1979, President Jimmy Carter made his famous "malaise" speech. The economy was not in recession. In the year preceding the speech, the economy grew by a solid 2.6 percent. But with productivity actually falling, real wages collapsing, and energy prices rising, negative feelings were pervasive. As Carter said at the time:

> It is a crisis of confidence. It is a crisis that strikes at the very heart and soul and spirit of our national will. The erosion of our confidence in the future is threatening to destroy the social and the political fabric of America. . . . We've learned that piling up material goods cannot fill the emptiness of lives which have no confidence or purpose. . . . For the first time in the history of our country a majority of our people believe that the next 5 years will be worse than the past 5 years.

This sort of pessimism found an echo in Japan after 10 years of sluggish growth. According to a 2002 Pew Survey, only 34 percent of Japanese were optimistic about their life improving over the next five years. The comparable figures were 65 percent in China, 57 percent in India, and 72 percent in Indonesia.

UNEMPLOYMENT, WAGES, AND DEBT

Just as a downshift to cautious growth is likely to hurt educated workers, more generally, a growth crisis will be associated with an increase in the overall unemployment rate, as it was in the U.S. in the 1970s and in Japan in the 1990s. The norm will become 6 percent unemployment or higher.

One group at particular risk is the young, who got hit especially hard in past growth crises. For example, in Japan in 2003, the rate of unemployment for people 15 to 24 stood at 10 percent–double what it was 10 years earlier. Similarly, a new growth crisis will hurt young Americans, who will have trouble getting good jobs.

As unemployment rises, suddenly the rapid debt growth of recent years will feel like a much heavier burden. From 2000 to the middle of 2003, consumers increased their mortgage and revolving debt by 26 percent, about double the increase in their disposable income. Part of that rise was justified by low interest rates and the refinancing of existing mortgage debt, which enabled Americans to borrow more without increasing interest payments.

However, Americans also borrowed assuming that their incomes would continue to rise in the future. There were plenty of people who pushed their borrowing to the limit in the hot housing market of recent years, expecting that rising incomes would bail them out. With a shift to cautious growth, those expectations of rising growth will just not be borne out. The result will be massive defaults on debts.

Student borrowers will be especially hard hit. As the cost of college has increased, more and more young people have been forced to take out enormous loans in order to pay for their education. And for most people, such borrowing has turned out to be worthwhile.

But for graduates coming out of college over the next few years, it could turn out to be the equivalent of buying at the top of a real estate bubble. The typical student debt burden for undergraduate education is heading toward $20,000. For law and medical degrees, the figure is closer to $90,000.

What's worse is that legislation passed in 1998 made it far more difficult to wipe out student loans by declaring bankruptcy.

All the people who took out big student loans will be stuck with them for the rest of their lives. It will weigh on this generation and the next.

Perhaps more important, the lack of growth would force the U.S. into a tough choice between "guns and butter." The U.S. is the biggest military spender globally by far, with the U.S. defense budget totaling more than six times the outlays of the next biggest spender, Russia. And it's the strength of the economy that has allowed the U.S. to construct the most potent military in history, without cutting back on civilian consumption. The growth spurt of the 1990s meant that GDP is about 7 percent bigger today than anyone expected. That's an additional $700 billion that can be split between military and civilian uses.

A key reason why the U.S. was able to fight a war in Iraq without financial help from its allies was the rapid growth of the economy. That extra $700 billion in GDP translates into at least an additional $120 billion in federal tax revenues, which is more than the cost of the Iraq war.

If productivity growth slows, it will become that much harder to maintain all of our obligations, both military and economic. The squeeze on resources will be that much greater. And the political fights over the budget will become even more intense, if you can imagine that.

THE RETIREMENT FAILURE

For years, the prophets of doom have been loudly warning of an approaching retirement disaster. There has been a steady stream of books, articles, and speeches proclaiming that the baby boomers are undersaving, that Social Security is running out of money, that the cost of medical care for the elderly is going to bankrupt the government, that we are all going to retire poor and homeless.

In the worst-case scenario, all the most distressing prophecies for the baby boomer retirement come true. With cautious growth, it's absolutely certain that the economic output of the U.S. 20 years from now will not be large enough to pay for the retirement of the boomers. It doesn't matter whether the current system of Social Security and Medicare is kept as is, privatized, or completely revamped. If growth slows, and the economic pie is not big enough, both retirees and the working generations will suffer.

Coda

We've reached a fork in the river of growth. Along one branch flows a continuation of the 1990s—fast-moving, turbulent, exhilarating. The combination of finance and technology, if we embrace it, is able to propel us forward at a rapid rate, without our quite knowing what is around the next bend.

Along the other branch lie more placid, slower-moving waters. This would not be a renunciation of technology, but rather a slackening of the pace of change. It would have certain economic consequences—namely, a standard of living not as high as it could have been—but in some ways would be easier and less challenging.

The choice is not just economic but technological, financial, moral, and political as well. How much change are we willing to accept? How much financial risk—and how many booms and busts—can we handle? What is our responsibility to the next generation and to the rest of the world? And are we able to muster the political will to simultaneously go for growth and to protect those hurt by it?

This book makes the case that the faster, more turbulent branch is the right one to choose. If we do make that choice, the future will indeed be better than we think.

References and Notes

PROLOGUE

xiv   "lengthy and uncomfortable transition period": Alan Blinder and Richard Quandt, "The Computer and the Economy," *Atlantic Monthly,* December 1997, p. 26.

xiv   "The conventional view . . .": Paul Krugman, "Speed Trap," *Slate,* December 1997.

CHAPTER 1

9   "Why can't we just . . .": Lee Gomes, "Investors Still Believe in the Magical Powers of Technology Stocks," *Wall Street Journal,* August 4, 2003, p. B1.

9   "Technological progress is like a fragile and vulnerable plant . . .": Joel Mokyr, *The Lever of Riches* (New York: Oxford University Press, 1990), p. 16.

CHAPTER 2

16   "New products, new industries . . .": Vannevar Bush, *Science, the Endless Frontier* (Washington, D.C.: U.S. Government Printing Office, 1945).

17   "Without novel and radical departures . . .": Mokyr, *Lever of Riches,* p. 13.

19   "electricity sightseers . . .": Jill Jonnes, *Empires of Light: Edison, Tesla, Westinghouse and the Race to Electrify the World* (New York: Random House, 2003), p. 65.

23   calculations of national income and spending . . . : Angus Maddison, "Quantifying and Interpreting World Development," The Colin Clark Lecture, University of Queensland, Australia, August 2003.

CHAPTER 3

32   "glittered in the sky . . .": Jonnes, *Empires of Light*, p. 268.

32   A recent study from the Brookings Institution . . . : Robert Litan and Alice Rivlin, *Beyond the Dot.coms* (Washington, D.C.: Brookings, 2001).

35   "Since at least the Book of Proverbs . . .": "Is the Saving Rate Really That Bad?" *Fortune*, November 7, 1988.

36   "Though the wealth of a country . . .": Adam Smith, *The Wealth of Nations* (New York: Random House, 1937), p. 71.

37   the percentage of paupers in the population: Jeffrey Williamson, *Did British Capitalism Breed Inequality?* (Boston: George Allen and Unwin, 1985), p. 23.

42   "pure, simple, social fun . . .": Daniel Henninger, "This Economy's Worst Sin Is That It's So Dull," *Wall Street Journal*, May 16, 2003, p. A8.

CHAPTER 4

48   "The great question is now at issue . . .": Thomas Malthus, *First Essay on the Principle of Population*, 1798 (London: MacMillan, 1926), p. 3.

49   "marginal to the pure theory . . .": Roger Backhouse, *The Ordinary Business of Life: A History of Economics from the Ancient World to the Twenty-first Century* (Princeton, N.J.: Princeton University Press, 2002), p. 183.

49   "when giant new industries have spent their force, . . .":

Alvin Hansen, presidential address to the American Economics Association, *American Economic Review,* March 1939, pp. 4, 11.

51 *Lost Prophets . . .* : Alfred Malabre, *Lost Prophets* (Boston: Harvard Business School, 1994).

51 *A Perilous Progress . . .* : Michael Bernstein, *A Perilous Progress* (Princeton, N.J.: Princeton University Press, 2001).

52 "Advances in any science or field . . .": Milton Friedman, *Capitalism and Freedom* (Chicago: University of Chicago Press, 1962), p. 157.

53 "The ability to raise our national saving rate . . .": In Martin Feldstein, ed., *American Economic Policy in the 1980s* (Chicago: University of Chicago Press, 1994), p. 77.

53 In 1997, the Brookings Institution . . . : Robert Reischauer (ed.), *Setting National Priorities* (Washington, DC: Brookings, 1997).

53 "Mainstream economists are exceptionally united . . .": Alan Blinder, "The Speed Limit," *The American Prospect,* September–October 1997.

54 "High technology is fashionable . . .": Paul R. Krugman, *Geography and Trade* (Cambridge, Mass.: MIT Press, 1991), p. 54.

54 "technological disappointment . . .": Paul Krugman, "Why Most Economists' Predictions Are Wrong," *Red Herring,* June 1998.

54 "30 years after the moon landings . . .": Paul Krugman, "When Did the Future Get So Boring?" *Fortune,* September 27, 1999, p. 42.

54 "technology is not a magic elixir . . .": Paul Krugman, "Nihon Keizai Shambles," *New York Times,* May 14, 2000, section 4, p. 15.

55 "the goal is not to explain . . .": N. Gregory Mankiw, "The Growth of Nations," *Brookings Papers on Economic Activity*, Vol. 1, 1995, p. 280.

55 successor to Paul Samuelson's classic text: I helped revise the 15th edition of the Samuelson textbook, but I was paid a lump sum and have no financial interest in its sales. *BusinessWeek* is part of McGraw-Hill, which of course publishes some important economics textbooks that compete with the ones named here.

55 "mechanized ice cream machine": N. Gregory Mankiw, *Principles of Macroeconomics*, 3rd ed. (Mason, Oh.: Thomson/South-Western, 2004), p. 74. If anything, Mankiw's *Principles of Microeconomics* contains even fewer mentions of technology.

55 fourth factor contributing to productivity: Ibid. p. 246.

56 "What does the future hold . . .": Ibid. p. 257.

56 "the average rate of productivity growth during the 1990s . . .": N. Gregory Mankiw in Jeffrey Frankel and Peter Orszag (eds.), *American Economic Policy in the 1990s* (Cambridge, Mass.: MIT Press, 2002), p. 29.

57 "the sources of strong productivity growth . . .": N. Gregory Mankiw, speech to the National Association for Business Economics, September 15, 2003.

57 "use of the internet and corporate intranets . . .": Martin Feldstein, "Why Is Productivity Growing Faster?" Paper presented at the annual meeting of the American Economics Association, 2003.

58 "dearth of new technology": William, J. Baumol and Alan S. Blinder, *Economics: Principles and Policy*, 9th ed. (Mason, Oh.: Thomson/South-Western, 2003), p. 270. It is fascinating to note that in his academic work, Baumol could well be classified as an advocate of innovation. For

example, in his 2002 book *The Free-Market Innovation Machine,* Baumol argues that "the most critical attribute of the free-market economy" may very well be "its ability to produce a stream of applied innovations and a rate of growth in living standards far beyond anything that any other economy has ever been able to achieve for any protracted period." However, virtually none of this emphasis on innovation gets transmitted to the student reading his textbook.

58   "Economy B, blessed by scientific and engineering discoveries . . .": Paul A. Samuelson, *Economics,* 11 ed. (New York: McGraw-Hill, 1980), pp. 21, 23.

59   "a culture of living within one's means": Horst Kohler, "Sustaining Global Growth and the Way Forward for Latin America," speech, Madrid, March 11, 2003.

59   "The best case for increased saving . . .": N. Gregory Mankiw, "Are We a Nation of Spendthrifts?" *Fortune,* February 15, 1999.

60   "One line of policy . . .": J. Bradford DeLong, Claudia Goldin, and Lawrence Katz, "Sustaining U.S. Economic Growth," *Agenda for the Nation* (Washington, D.C.: Brookings Institution, 2003), p. 47.

60   "correlation between equipment investment and growth . . .": Jonathan Temple, "The New Growth Evidence," *Journal of Economic Literature,* March 1999, pp. 138–139.

61   increases in capital investment by themselves don't add much to growth: What about investment in education? Roughly speaking, investment in education has about the same rate of return as investment in physical capital–about 10 percent a year–so it has the same relatively meager impact on long-term growth.

61   "debt fairy": Douglas Elmendorf and N. Gregory Mankiw, "Government Debt," *Handbook of Macroeconomics 1999* (New York: Elsevier, 1999), p. 1633.

61   "positive effect on growth is weak . . .": Robert J. Barro, *Determinants of Economic Growth* (Cambridge, Mass.: MIT Press, 1997), p. 35.

61   even large changes in the government budget deficit: Alice Rivlin and Isabel Sawhill (eds.), *Restoring Fiscal Sanity: How to Balance the Budget* (Washington, D.C.: Brookings Institution, 2004), pp. x, 9.

62   "personal retirement accounts": Martin Feldstein and Andrew Samwick, "Maintaining Social Security Benefits and Tax Rates Through Personal Retirement Accounts: An Update," NBER Working Paper No. 6540, March 1, 1999, p. 10.

62   "Although growth theory implied . . .": Feldstein, *American Economic Policy*, p. 16.

63   "No one yet knows enough . . .": DeLong, Goldin, and Katz, p. 45.

CHAPTER 5

67   "consequences of our ingenuity": Elting Morison, *Men, Machines, and Modern Times* (Cambridge, Mass.: MIT Press, 1966), p. 43.

69   "There was nothing scientific . . .": Robert Rubin and Jacob Weisberg, *In an Uncertain World* (New York: Random House, 2003), p. 121.

69   Out of about 150 Fleeces . . . : Robert Irion, "What Proxmire's Golden Fleece Did for–and to–Science," *The Scientist*, December 12, 1988.

70   "violated the basic moral principle . . .": Benjamin

Friedman, *Day of Reckoning: The Consequences of American Economic Policy under Reagan and After* (New York: Random House, 1988), p. 4.

71 "this literature has typically supported . . .": Elmendorf and Mankiw, p. 1658.

72 "It is clear that job losers . . .": Henry Farber, "Job Loss in the United States, 1981–2001," NBER Working paper No. 9707, May 2003, p. 32.

73 "what seemed to be the dawn of a new era . . .": Joseph E. Stiglitz, *The Roaring Nineties: A New History of the World's Most Prosperous Decade* (New York: W. W. Norton, 2003), p. 3.

73 "The belief in technological determinism . . .": Jeffrey Madrick, *Why Economies Grow: The Forces That Shape Prosperity and How We Can Get Them Working Again* (New York: Basic Books, 2002), p. 13.

74 "The new era came with a real world price tag . . .": Thomas Frank, *One Market under God: Extreme Capitalism, Market Populism, and the End of Economic Democracy* (New York: Doubleday, 2000), p. 356–357.

74 "The great euphoria of the late nineties . . .": Ibid. p. 358.

74 "the frontiers of development of science . . .": Robert M. Collins, *More: The Politics of Economic Growth in Postwar America* (New York: Oxford University Press, 2000), p. 5.

74 "Our industrial plant is built": Ibid. p. 5.

75 "The emphasis of so many New Deal programs . . .": Ibid. p. 6.

76 "economy of abundance": Quoted in ibid. p. 63.

77 "a genie that capitalism let out of the bottle . . .": Robert L. Heilbroner and James K. Galbraith, *The Economic Problem*, 9th ed. (Englewood Cliffs, N.J.: Prentice-Hall, 1990), p. 24.

77 "the new technology brings unprecedented threats": Ibid. p. 424.

77 "the sharp rise in inner-city joblessness . . .": William Julius Wilson, *When Work Disappears* (New York: Knopf, 1996), p. 151.

79 "a culture without a moral foundation . . .": Neil Postman, *Technopoly* (New York: Alfred A. Knopf, 1992), p. xii.

79 "Unlike more moral pursuits . . .": Jerry Z. Muller, *The Mind and the Market: Capitalism in Modern European Thought* (New York: Alfred A. Knopf, 2002), p. 5.

80 "wealth was an act of fortuitous circumstance . . .": Joseph Finkelstein and Alfred L. Thimm, *Economists and Society: Development of Economic Thought from Aquinas to Keynes* (New York: Harper & Row, 1973), p. 8.

81 "Knowledge and innovation grow at breathtaking rates . . .": Daniel Sarewitz, *Frontiers of Illusion: Science Technology, and the Politics of Progress* (Philadelphia: Temple University Press, 1996), p. 3.

81 "Is it possible that our technological reach . . .": Bill McKibben, *Enough: Staying Human in an Engineered Age* (New York: Times Books, 2003), p. xii.

81 "The invention of the car . . .": Ibid. p. 45.

83 "The potential of new technologies and policies . . .": *State of the World 2002*, Worldwatch Institute (New York: W. W. Norton, 2002), p. 30.

83 "A hydrogen fuel-cell car . . .": Amory Lovins, "Twenty Hydrogen Myths," Rocky Mountain Institute, September 2003.

84 "The precautionary principle requires . . .": Mae Wan Ho, "The Precautionary Principle Is Coherent," Institute of Science in Society, October 31, 2000.

84 "decided to eat their food raw": *Scientific American,* January 2001, p. 18.

85 "To drop a new and far-reaching technology . . .": Daniel Callahan, *What Price Better Health? Hazards of the Research Imperative* (Berkeley, Calif.: University of California Press, 2003), p. 84.

85 "There is no reason whatever . . .": Ibid. pp. 83–84.

86 "is not only unnecessary but ruinous": Aleksandr Solzhen-itsyn, *Letter to the Soviet Leaders* (New York: Harper and Row, 1974), p. 22.

86 "The steady state view . . .": Herman Daly, *Steady State Economics* (San Francisco: W. H. Freeman, 1977), p. 46.

CHAPTER 6

92 "Pervasive uncertainty characterizes . . .": Nathan Rosen-berg, "Uncertainty and Technological Change," *Technology and Growth,* Federal Reserve Bank of Boston, Conference Series, No. 40, June 1996.

93 information technology predictions . . . : Herman Kahn and Anthony Wiener, *The Year 2000* (New York: MacMillan, 1967) p. 51.

94 another set of technology forecasts . . . : Herman Kahn, *The Coming Boom* (New York: Simon & Schuster, 1982), p. 67.

96 "Macroinventions . . . do not . . .": Mokyr, p. 13.

97 "most TV ads will have URLs . . .": Kathy Rebello, "Inside Microsoft," *BusinessWeek,* July 15, 1996, p. 56.

98 "We thought it might have some communications and scientific uses . . .": Arthur Schawlow, http://www.bell-labs.com/news/1999/april/30/1.html.

100 Europe leads in 12 scientific fields: R. D. Shelton and Geoffrey Holdridge, "The U.S.-EU Race for Leadership of Science and Technology," Loyola College, 2003.

104 chronic and debilitating conditions: J. D. Kleinke, "The Price of Progress," *Health Affairs*, September/October 2001.

104 "treatment expansion effect": David Cutler and Mark McClellan, "Is Technological Change in Medicine Worth It?" *Health Affairs*, September/October 2001.

109 start-ups such as Nanosolar . . . : Elizabeth Corcoran, "Bright Ideas," *Forbes*, November 24, 2003, p. 222.

109 "Absent other incentives . . .": "Fuel Cell Report to Congress," Department of Energy, February 2003, p. vi.

111 cost of nuclear power . . . : "The Future of Nuclear Power," Massachusetts Institute of Technology, 2003, p. 7.

113 "This nation . . .": John F. Kennedy, speech to Congress, May 25, 1961.

CHAPTER 7

116 "invariably ossify and decline": Raghuram G. Rajan and Luigi Zingales, *Saving Capitalism from the Capitalists* (New York: Crown Business, 2003), p. 1.

117 feedback loops . . . : Robert Shiller, *Irrational Exuberance* (Princeton, N.J.: Princeton University Press, 2000), p. 44.

120 encyclopedic study of venture capital: Paul Gompers and Josh Lerner, *The Money of Invention* (Cambridge, Mass.: Harvard Business School Press, 2001).

121 the failure rate for venture-backed companies: Ibid. p. 21.

122 three times as many patents: Ibid. p. 76.

129 "Wal-Mart directly and indirectly . . .": "U.S. Productivity Growth 1995–2000," McKinsey Global Institute, 2001.

CHAPTER 8

133   "Expectations can be quickly altered": Charles Kindleberger, *Manias, Panics, and Crashes* (New York: Basic
Books, 1978), p. 113.

134   "Investment must often be made on a daring hunch . . .":
Alvin Hansen, *Business Cycles and National Income,* rev. ed.
(New York: W.W. Norton, 1964), pp. 139–40.

135   "almost surely an illusion": Alan Greenspan "Economic
Volatility" speech at Jackson Hole, Wyoming, August 30,
2002.

135   "Central bankers should not willfully ignore
developments . . .": Stephen G. Cecchetti, Brandeis
University, "Central Bankers and Asset Price
Misalignments," May 2002.

CHAPTER 9

144   "Boston to the moon": Frederick A. Cleveland and Fred
Wilbur Powell, *Railroad Promotion and Capitalization in
the United States* (New York: Johnson Reprint Corp., 1966;
reprint of 1909 edition), p. 76.

145   required railroads to pay tolls: Ibid. p. 74.

145   "sensitive to the political winds": Rajan and Zingales,
p. 3.

147   "predatory minority enriched itself . . .": Louis Koenig,
Bryan (New York: Putnam, 1971), p. 137.

CHAPTER 10

159   In a 1977 survey . . . : Nancy Ochsner and Lewis Solmon,
College Education and Employment (Bethlehem, Penn.:
CPC Foundation, 1979), p. 85.

159   "a marginal rather than highly profitable endeavor": Richard Freeman, *The Overeducated American* (New York: Academic Press, 1976), p. 4.

159   "slowing down": Jerome Wiesner, "Has the U.S. Lost Its Initiative in Technological Innovation?" *Technology Review,* July–August 1976, p. 60.

159   "Vanishing Innovation": *BusinessWeek,* July 3, 1978, p. 46.

162   "the ideal of the liberal college education . . .": Leonard Nakamura, "Education and Training in an Era of Creative Destruction" (Federal Reserve Bank of Philadelphia, March 2001).

164   "routine tasks": David H. Autor, Frank Levy, and Richard J. Murnane, "The Skill Content of Recent Technological Change," *Quarterly Journal of Economics,* 118(4) (November 2003).

165   "The idea that technological advances favor more skilled workers . . .": Daron Acemoglu, "Technical Change, Inequality, and the Labor Market," *Journal of Economic Literature,* March 2002, p. 8.

CHAPTER 11

171   "only for growth to collapse later on": Jonathan Temple, "The New Growth Evidence," *Journal of Economic Literature,* March 1999, p. 116.

171   "History does raise some warning flags . . .": Alan Greenspan, "Productivity" speech in Washington, D.C., October 23, 2002.

176   The typical student debt burden . . . : "National Student Loan Survey," Nellie Mae Corporation, February 6, 2003.

Index